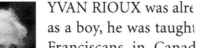 YVAN RIOUX was alre
as a boy, he was taught
Franciscans in Canada. He studied biology at
Montreal University, but it left him cold as it didn't
touch anything that was alive. Working for ten years
as a biodynamic farmer in Quebec, however, he encountered many
living ecosystems. Later, in Montreal, he taught on the relationship between human physiology and nature. In 1992 he moved
to England with his two boys and joined a family of two girls and
their mother, Gabriel Millar, who became his muse. Retiring ten
years ago, he decided to write about his knowledge gained from
25 years' of teaching experience, culminating in his previous pub-
lication, *The Mystery of Emerging Form* (2017).

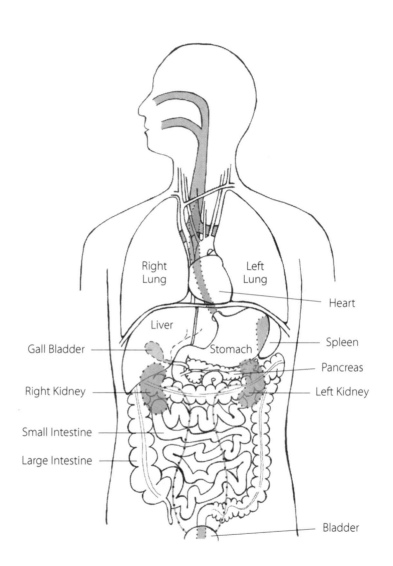

THE SEAT OF THE SOUL

Rudolf Steiner's Seven Planetary Seals

A BIOLOGICAL PERSPECTIVE

YVAN RIOUX

TEMPLE LODGE

Temple Lodge Publishing Ltd.
Hillside House, The Square
Forest Row, RH18 5ES

www.templelodge.com

First published by Temple Lodge Publishing, 2018

A CIP catalogue record for this book is available from the British Library

ISBN 978 1 912230 23 5

Cover by DesignIsIdentity.com
Images: janez volmajer (stars), Anusorn Nakdee (vortex),
Embargo (drop), all shutterstock.com

Typesetting by DesignIsIdentity.com
Printed and bound by 4Edge Ltd., Essex

Contents

Chapter 6: Venus process:
Energized movements for growth
A constant search for the right fulcrum point   178

Chapter 7: Moon process:
Replication (mitosis vs meiosis)
Self-renewing life   208

Conclusion
A planetary alignment giving birth
to our physical and psychic world   220

Acknowledgements

Many thanks

to my wife, the writer Gabriel Millar, who ruthlessly edited and opened me to the grammar and beauty of the English language (my mother-tongue is French),

to my son, Mathieu, the patient computer wizard, who provided inestimable instruction in the technology, and for his brilliant contribution to the organization of the text and the coherence of the drawings,

to the artist and lover of trees, Fred Hageneder for his tireless artistic input on the making of the book,

to my friend, Peter Stephenson, for our never-ending discussions about spiritual science where the thinking process is fed not only by outer perceptions but, more importantly, by inner ones,

to the poet Jay Ramsay who gave me the title whilst discussing Novalis,

and numerous other companions and students for their encouragement in gathering this biological perspective on human physiology.

Introduction

Beyond the static state

For millennia human perception of the Cosmos led us to believe that our Earth was the static centre of the Universe and that every star revolved around us in an orderly and dynamic way. German astronomer, Nicolaus Copernicus (1473 – 1543) was one of the first to challenge this notion and posited instead that the Sun must be the centre of the Universe around which our Earth orbits. We now know that the Earth or indeed the Sun are not static centres, indeed, we do not know if such a thing as a static centre exists anywhere in the Universe. Cosmological models developed in the twentieth century refer to a homogeneous and coherent Universe which lacks a central static point. It seems that everything in the Universe is on the move all the time.

From the double helix of DNA in each of our own cells to the vast Milky Way Galaxy where the Solar System resides, there are constant motions that bring changes everywhere; transformation is the rule. Throughout Human history, many religions would view life after death as an eternally static state of ecstasy or punishment. If we observe that change, movement and evolution is the norm in the physical world, why should we assume a static state awaits us after death?

Are we now in a time in history when we can accept the possibility that the physical, psychic and spiritual worlds are part of the same reality in co-evolution? That our spiritual aspects are not simply transferred to a static 'Heaven' or 'Hell' at the point of physical death but that this spiritual part of our being can also change and evolve just like our physical selves? That it too must be impacted by the constant rhythmic motions of the Universe? Some philosophies embrace this idea with concepts like reincarnation etc...

Ancient Indian and Egyptian societies had their complex interpretations of life after death. More recently in the Western world many have revived some of these ideas. Notably, Austrian philosopher and scientist, Rudolf Steiner (1861 – 1925) was responsible for providing an account of a more dynamic interpretation of our involvement with the Spirit world.

Planetary movements

The Earth orbits the Sun in 'more or less' one year. It rotates on a 'wobbly' axis in 'approximately' 24 hours and pulses twice a day with 'variable' tides. Nothing is static or constant; even Earth's polar alignment and magnetic field are on the move when viewed over geological periods.

The words 'more or less', 'approximately', 'wobbly' and 'variable' are to emphasise the fact that these movements are not neatly regular. When mathematics is used to grasp them, all must relate with the concept of infinity. One conclusion we can draw from this is the simple thought that we are living not in a strictly *mechanical system* but a highly complex *dynamic system* linked with infinity. It cannot be comprehended in its entirety with mathematical reasoning alone.

Rudolf Steiner sought to bring our attention to this important fact and its vital role in life on Earth:

> It is easy to agree that this mutability of the eccentric orbits, and of the mutual inclination of the planes of the orbits must, somehow or other, be connected with the life of the whole planetary system, or shall we say, with its continuing activity. It must be connected in some way with the living activity of the whole planetary system.... *One finds that the reason why the system has not actually reached rigidity under the influence of the disturbance—the variability of the nodes, etc.—is that the ratios of the period of revolution of the planets are not commensurable.* They are incommensurable quantities, numbers with decimals to an infinite number of places. Thus we may say, if we compare the periods of revolution of the planets in the sense of Kepler's law: the ratio of these periods cannot be given in integers, nor in finite fractions, but only in incommensurable numbers.
>
> RUDOLF STEINER (1)

We live on a planet whose intrinsic movements are difficult to perceive or predict. The more we observe, the longer cycles and patterns we find—the precession of the equinoxes, for instance, takes 25,920 years to complete one cycle.

Earth's rotational axis is more or less oriented towards the North Star (Stella Polaris). Its circuit around the Sun is about 365 days. Actually it is more like 365.24...days. This is why we have to add one day in February every four years to catch up with this starry dynamic clock. The Earth pulses with its two tidal movements every day. The electrons in all matter, which are made up of congealed light particles that pulse and rotate around a centre close to the speed of light, have a similar motion.

We can never pinpoint specifically the elliptical motion of the planets around the Sun. The number for the velocity of each planet always relates to the concept of infinity in mathematics. Even to calculate the surface of a circle or the volume of a sphere, we need Pi, which is 22/7. If we do the division we end up with 3.1415...till infinity. Any movement in our Solar System is always an approximation that extends to infinity (2).

Our whole Solar System travels within the Milky Way Galaxy which is itself moving towards the constellation of Hercules at a speed of 500,000 km per hour! With all these movements Earth continually loses some matter to space. To compensate, showers of matter (meteoric iron and particles such as those which form the aurora borealis) rain down to Earth every day (hundreds of tons per day).

The vast magnetic field of the Earth attracts various charged particles and directs them towards the poles where they enter the Earth. And then what happens to these particles? Many of them penetrate matter very easily and so are very difficult to detect. Do they eventually stop within the Earth or go through our planet untransformed? Or is there a digestion process at the centre of the Earth where new matter is produced and pushes its way out through the strata? Is the Earth growing? Is it filtering these particles and sending them back out into space?

Over aeons the continents of the Earth have moved up, down and sideways through the actions of the tectonic plates. These geological movements often drag surface deposits underground where enormous pressure is exerted on them generating metamorphic rock (transforming clay into slate, for instance).

New tectonic plate surface is always being generated at the mid-ocean ridges which changes the profile of the Earth. In a human lifetime we notice some of these rumblings as earthquakes. Volcanic activity is also a big factor in this general shake-up of matter, bringing deep liquid rocks to the surface as well as dust and gaseous substances into the atmosphere.

We know hardly anything of what is below the solid rock of the Earth's crust, just working hypotheses. We also know very little about the movement of water in that crust. In several kilometres of crust there must be entire rivers and underground seas on the move even from one continent to another. That water emerges as springs with specific ratios of minerals, sometimes hot and sulphuric, or as rhythmic effusions (geysers) indicating a connection with mysterious deep hot layers under the crust.

Air and water in our atmosphere also have their powerful motions, sometimes dangerous and capricious (such as in tornadoes and hurricanes). Jet streams in the atmosphere around the poles and the vast undersea currents such as the Gulf Stream contribute to the general exchange of substances. Everything in space is constantly in motion; there is no resting place but just temporary immobility.

As a body in space, the Earth receives from the cosmos a myriad of electromagnetic radiations across the whole spectrum from radio frequencies to elusive cosmic rays. Like all living creatures, the Earth has many complex membranes which have filtering and digestive properties. In Earth's case, these membranes are atmospheric (e.g. Ozone). These are in a constant state of movement, coming close to the Earth and retreating like pulsating envelopes (3). If we think that these rhythmic pulsing movements have no effect on us we misinterpret their constant influence on our internal environment.

The other thing concerning this shake-up of various states of matter is the fact that there is a constant striving towards an equilibrium of substances that are favourable for the expression of Life. In this study of our internal self-enclosed body we will repeatedly find these negative bio-feedback loops in constant search for the right fulcrum point of balance for Life. In *Gaia*, British scientist James Lovelock (1919 –) is quite eloquent about the dynamic systems ruling the strict concentration of various substances such as oxygen in the air or salts in sea water which effectively make Earth a self-regulating system. German scientist, Johann Wolfgang von Goethe (1749 – 1832) also refers to Earth or Nature as a single entity:

> The one thing she [Nature] seems to aim at is individuality; yet she cares nothing for individuals. She is always building up and destroying; but her workshop is inaccessible.
>
> JOHANN WOLFGANG VON GOETHE (4)

In the womb of pulsed motion

It is important that we understand how much effect the constant rhythmic pulsing motion from the Universe has on all living systems on Earth. The larger impacts of heat, light and gravity from the Sun and Moon are obvious and easily measurable by science but these bodies and all others in the Solar System also affect us in more subtle ways. They not only have an impact on living beings physically but they are also instrumental in shaping the internal organization of all life on Earth.

As discussed in my previous book, *The Mystery of Emerging Form* (2017), the external form of living beings emerges out of movements of contraction and expansion under the guidance of formative forces (architects) from the 12 Constellations (5).

As for our internal forms (organs) and their metabolic processes, they are more greatly influenced by the movements of the main planets in our Solar System, what Steiner called the Planetary Spheres. This is the subject of this book.

The movements of our neighbouring planets over years viewed from the Earth, from a geocentric vantage, is a constant dance with beautiful patterns. The Earth, like the other planets, orbits the Sun on an elliptical path. If we observe any of the planets over a period of time, they will appear to periodically move closer and further away and will paint a regular geometric pattern in the night sky (see Figure 1). This pulsed motion impacts on the diverse landscapes of our internal organs.

There is no real separation between the outside world and the inside of living creatures but a *constant reverberation of resonance.* (6)

Figure 1: Venus orbit as seen from Earth. Each planet forms a different geometric shape.

Forms always prompt a response in our soul. Every atom, plant molecular architecture and structural protein radiate their own identifying energy patterns. Every material structure, natural or man-made, emanates a unique energy signature. The Empire State Building or Chartres Cathedral generate different responses in our soul.

This book looks at human physiology and aims to correspond the outside rhythmic motions of Nature and the Planetary Spheres with our inner organs that are an ever-pulsing summary of what is outside. Consequently, studying human physiology helps us understand the physiology of Nature and vice versa.

This study is not about malfunction or disease. Every living entity has a dedication to maintain a state of equilibrium, because life is always a knife-edge experience. So here we will describe the

Human organs in their healthy states. Living beings have a drive to unfold their internal and external forms, as well as their psyches, in a state of balance with their surroundings.

IMPORTANT NOTE
The word 'process' as an abstract concept will be used often. Rudolf Steiner suggested that it should be pictured as an unfolding, unwinding rhythm.

A special alignment of planetary spheres

The Planetary Spheres sequence used in this text doesn't contradict the Copernicus system: the Sun at the centre with three outer planets and three inner planets (or two planets and our moon, to be precise). According to Rudolf Steiner this sequence is more auspicious to grasp the seven stages of our metabolic process. After all it is from this sequence that our physical and psychic worlds emerge progressively.

Saturn – Jupiter – Mars – Sun – Mercury – Venus – Moon

And this was the sequence contemplated by an old instinctive wisdom. Because this order appeared important [to understand our inner physiology].

RUDOLF STEINER (7)

Note that other planetary objects in the Solar System such as Uranus, Neptune and Pluto are not included in this sequence—Rudolf Steiner states that these outer bodies have a lesser impact on internal organ formation and development and have more impact on our psyche.

A progressive understanding of the alignment of the seven heavenly bodies listed above will emerge through the reading of this book.

We live inside a greater organism—the Solar System. Here we look at the impact of the Planetary Spheres on the formation of our soma (physical body) and psychic world. The expression

'Planetary Spheres' is used to show the geocentric point of view where the planets, the Sun and our Moon revolve around the Earth as we experience it. Because the Earth moves at the same time as the planets, the Earth observer sees interesting and beautifully ordered patterns in their trajectory over the years (Figure 1 above). See (2) for recommended reading on our Solar System.

These choreographic signatures reflect as activities in us and were called by the ancients the Music of the Spheres. It was Greek philosopher Pythagoras of Samos (570 – 495 BC) who whilst studying the relationship between a musical note and the string that produces it first suggested that the celestial bodies must also emit their own unique tone based on their orbit. Subsequently, Greek philosopher Plato (428 – 347 BC) describes Music and Astronomy as 'paired' subjects which are closely related by their mathematical proportions.

It is incorrect to think that the planets are too small or far away to have an influence on Life on Earth. The Sun and the Moon have a clear, easily measurable influence. Any celestial body must also have an influence correspondingly scaled by factors of mass and distance. Of course here we are talking of subtle, spiritual morphic influences, formative and pictorial, which are creating our internal micro-cosmos and are ever present within us.

The seven chapters of this book explore the etheric aspect of the human body and how the pulsing penetration of the outside world forges our inner physiology as well as our psychic make-up. Both of these are always mobile and inter-connected. That the Earth is part of a living Solar System is the assumption here. We are not attached to this elliptical planetary system simply by the force of gravity.

And what is gravity anyway? This was one of German theoretical physicist Albert Einstein's (1879 – 1955) biggest problems. He was never able to unite this force with the others in his general theory of relativity.

In *The Mystery of Emerging Form* (2017), I describe how the twelve constellations of the Milky Way induce twelve archetypal tendencies to form elements to complete the outer human form.

In this book, we will see the seven Planetary Spheres unfold seven life steps that progressively produce our inner make-up (both physical and psychic).

> And in his etheric body man lives in different ways in these (seven) different life-stages.
>
> RUDOLF STEINER (8)

The seven chapters follow Rudolf Steiner's approach, making a start with Saturn as the most outward planet with a direct effect on our metabolic processes. There is an alignment of metabolic influences starting from the entry of the outer world into us. First in the sequence of Planetary Spheres, Saturn influences the life of senses, with the Moon as the last in the sequence, representing the life of reproduction, the capacity for another spirit to come into incarnation.

The relation between the planets and the way they reverberate in organ systems was known by the ancient Chinese. We will see in this study how Rudolf Steiner's approach is very similar to ancient Chinese physiology; both are concerned with how the external and internal environments interact as activity—outside as an image of inside.

The reverberation of the planetary forces in organs regulates our sense of wellbeing. What are their embryonic beginnings, their fulcrum point of activity, their impact on the blood stream and their role in the activities of our psyche as a tool of expression? We will explore these questions.

Steiner produced geometric representations of each of the Planetary Spheres which he called 'Seals'. In this context, what do Steiner's seven seals teach us? Each planet has traditionally been associated with a metal. What is the subtle role of that planetary metal on our physiology? There is in us a constant pulse of condensation and rarefaction of metals. It seems that when a substance is rarefied it acts as an activity holding some oscillating properties. There would be no harmonious metabolic processes without them.

Note 1:
Rudolf Steiner and Traditional Chinese physiology

In the first decades of the twentieth century Rudolf Steiner endeavoured to give new impulses concerning all levels of human activity. He observed at that time a growing materialistic tendency to explain the world exclusively with perceptible matter and its measurable energies. He taught and lectured on many subjects, from agriculture to architecture, from a new way to perceive the Christ event to our relation with the Beings of the living cosmos we are nested in. He suggested a more healthy threefold social order and spoke of the evolution of the soul through reincarnation; he coherently touched many aspects of the human condition.

This book focuses on the impulses given by Steiner to help us grasp the complexity of the human being and its constant relation with the surrounding Universe. Through several lectures, summarized in his book *An Occult Physiology* (1911) he presented a totally new approach to the health of internal activities and their possible dysfunctions. He also warned his audience, several times, not to take him at face value. What he said was knowledge for him but for us it is information that we need to verify for ourselves. He emphasized the fact that an effort is needed to integrate these new impulses that counteract the tendency to perceive human beings simply as complex machines.

This effort can be greatly helped by studying traditional Chinese texts on the subject. Chinese medicine goes back to a few millennia before Christ. Take a western example: When Homer wrote *The Iliad* and *The Odyssey* he was writing down an oral tradition that had been passed down for centuries. The capacity to hold the memory of the past through storytelling was phenomenal in those days. Homer was the first to write it down, just as the brothers Grimm were the first to collect ancient Germanic fairy tales. The same thing happened in ancient China.

During the Shang dynasty (fourteenth to eleventh century before Christ) the first evidence of texts appeared describing Chinese medicine. These texts took the form of a dialogue with the Yellow Emperor and related how the human being interacted with his pulsing environment. Over the centuries practitioners added their comments concerning this fragile equilibrium we call health, and developed various healing techniques from herbal to dietary prescriptions, from acupuncture to revitalizing exercises, like qigong.

Their voluminous physiological texts focused mainly on the etheric activity that generates and maintains the physical body (soma) with its impact on the soul (psyche). Because they were describing complex circulatory movements between outside and inside, and their inter-relations, their form of writing with ideograms (pictures) was perfectly apt. The force that gives motion to objects and processes they called ch'i or qi. I shall refer to it as CHI in this text. They identified currents of CHI energy and called these channels meridians that connect the skin with all our internal organs. They learned to increase or decrease these currents through stimulation with needles or pressure.

In this book the expression *'liquid light'* or ether current is a metaphor for that very individualised ZHEN CHI that each person is continually creating and which circulates in channels across the body called meridians. Every chapter will touch on this subject from a different angle because all the subtle aspects of the five organ systems are involved in the creation and movement of CHI.

Occult Physiology by Rudolf Steiner and the ancient Chinese point of view

This book is an attempt to penetrate the various new impulses that Rudolf Steiner gave to medicine concerning our complex inner make-up. His intention was to help his contemporaries to overcome an increasingly materialistic way of thinking. By building a picture of human physiology that goes beyond our strict sense perception, he invited us to apprehend the invisible intelligent activity that creates us. This is the supersensible (see *An Occult Physiology* by Rudolf Steiner).

In following his invitation to see behind the physical, we can also be greatly helped by the way traditional Chinese physiologists saw the body's inner organization in relation to the highly pulsed activity of Nature and the Cosmos.

When they tried to grasp the activity of an organ, the Chinese looked for a 'landscape'—a functional area impacting on biological and psychic processes. They wrote down their findings with ideograms. It is worth mentioning at this stage that the ideograms we are going to translate don't belong to the realm of rigid concept. They are images that try to grasp a subtle reality of forces behind the perceptible world and are best apprehended by a mobile form of thinking rather than one which seeks mainly fixed relations between fixed entities.

This book in no way exhausts this vast subject: the comprehension that Rudolf Steiner and the ancient Chinese had of the relationship between the vibrant outside world and our mobile inner bubble will still be studied for centuries to come. The ideograms of the five main organs (liver, heart, spleen, lung and kidney) and the five daily and seasonal movements (HUA) set out in the Wu Xing of Chinese medicine will be partially explored here. (8)

When considering our inner organs, we find different organ types with specific functions. Some organs tend to be hollow and are designed to separate the good stuff from what we don't need. They are excretory. They are called *Workshop organs* in Chinese physiology and are seen as YANG, meaning directional, transformative organs (e.g. the colon). They process the internal liquids, as well as what is coming from food, by separating what we need and don't need for our ideal equilibrium.

Other organs tend to give a direction to the blood stream. They are called *Treasure organs* and seen as YIN meaning receptive, listening organs (e.g. the lungs). Treasure and Workshop organs are energetically linked through the flow of liquid light in the meridians in a circadian rhythm.

In Europe, ancient Greek philosophers also looked at Nature in terms of processes. When describing the Elements (Earth, Water, Air, Fire), they did not mean elements as we understand them (the 92 elements of the Periodic Table) but were describing the states of matter of these elements: the three states (solid, liquid, gas) governed by a fourth one—heat. Each terrestrial state was united with a peripheric cosmic ether perceived as intelligent activity linked with each state. Rudolf Steiner made a great contribution to the understanding of the states of matter and their ethers, and this will be described in this text.

Today in Physics we use the term plasma for another state of matter. In fact, what is meant is a subset of the gas state where part of the electrons has been stripped away, making the atoms positive. In this condition electric or magnetic fields can act on them. Solar flares, the ionosphere or even a simple fluorescent bulb are plasma phenomena. 99% of the space between the stars is in a plasma state with ions and ionized particles of all kinds, such as gamma or cosmic rays. Outer space, between the stars, is far from empty.

Ancient Chinese tradition, aware of the qualities of the sectors of space, focused on the five HUA or the pulsing recurring movements of days and seasons in the progress of the Earth around the Sun. We shall see how these influences, through a process in time, foster a threefold manifestation in living beings on Earth. These HUA have a profound effect on the creation of the natural living world, as well as on our inner cosmos of organs. This constant increase and decrease of light and heat on a daily and seasonal basis manifests in manifold ways as the activator of all organic activities on Earth. These ideograms were mobile ideas referring to an activity. In translation they become concepts, WOOD –

FIRE – EARTH – METAL – WATER. The activity which each one reflects is better expressed as image or ideogram. In the same way that the Greek 'elements' are really referring to a state of matter rather than a physical element, these Chinese HUA should be viewed as representing a process rather than a physical object.

IMPORTANT NOTE
All Chinese HUA will be in capital letters in the text, while the Greek Elements, representing the four States of matter with their specific Ether activities, will have the first letter capitalized. So in this text, water (rain), Water (one of the Greek Elements that means the liquid state of matter with its chemical/sound ether) and WATER (one of the five HUA that means a movement of contraction like night or winter or a seed returning to its point origin) are three different things.

These five HUA, describing the constant contraction and expansion of Nature in time, have a profound effect on plant and animal development. Plants, which have a threefold architecture of root, stem/leaf and flower, always develop through contraction and expansion. This is the way the etheric forces operate. The threefoldness of living plants develops through a time process.

Note 2:
Plant Becoming—A Carbohydrate Architecture

Observing plant development through space and time we can't miss the constant movement of contraction and expansion which is the way the etheric builds up living creatures.

1 – It always starts with a contracted **point**, be it a seed or a bud waiting for the right condition to unfold. HUA—WATER

2 – Germination produces **line** expressions going downward (root) towards the Earth (geotropism) and going upward (stem) towards the Sun (heliotropism). HUA—WOOD

3 – From these lines leaf **surfaces** will emerge (cotyledons or first leaves) that progressively unfold. Each time a leaf

appears (expansion), it is always accompanied by a bud (contraction). Under the ground the roots form a matrix of lines that invades the richest aspect of the soil inviting the bacterial world to cooperate in extracting the best nutrients for the species. HUA—FIRE

4 – Progressive unfolding of the leaves through a constant contraction and expansion allows the plant to establish itself in space. This unfoldment tends to go anti-clockwise along the growing stem with changes in the leaf shape that tends to decrease in size. HUA—FIRE

5 – Suddenly, another metamorphosis occurs. A group of leaves (flower bud) expands into a flower **volume (sepals and petals)** giving rise to organs of reproduction, contracting into the pistil and stamen. A new expansion brings pollen and aroma into the surrounding, favouring the meeting of male and female gametes. This allows the mingling of genes. Under the ground, in some species, we see tubers (potato, carrot) with budding eyes (contraction) that allows a vegetative reproduction for the next year (cloning). HUA— EARTH

6 – Through this fertilization a cluster of seeds (contraction) is produced.

7 – Sometimes a new expansion occurs in the form of pulpous fruit around the seeds (i.e. an orange).

8 – The maturation and drying of seeds leads towards the scattering (expansion) by air, water or animals. HUA—METAL

9 – A lot of nutritious seeds will be eaten by animals, but the ones falling onto auspicious soil—this fruitful womb (contraction)—will wait for the right time to germinate—starting a new cycle. Return to HUA—WATER

NB. The stem buds with their internal meristem cells (plant stem cells) will differentiate according to where they are. In many plants (vines) if the buds are in the dark moist soil they produce roots with searching, growing end buds, whereas in light dry air, they rhythmically unfold their leaves and flowers.

Animals are affected by these developmental forces in the same way. The physical centres of threefoldness show, in animals, in the appearance of head, thorax and abdomen holding centres for neuro-sensorial, rhythmic and metabolic functions (including limbs). These centres lead towards psychic centres for the faculties of thinking, feeling and willing. The psyche develops its own somatic foundation to emerge as a conscious inner world and marks the development of the astral body which distances us from the plant kingdom.

Our complex inner landscape of organs and processes is controlled automatically by a part of our nervous system that is relatively independent from our consciousness. It is formed of numerous 'little brains' (nervous ganglia) spread all over our body and is called the autonomic nervous system (ANS). The ANS is responsible for regulating our body's unconscious actions.

Biologists recognize two main divisions of the autonomic nervous system that strive for homoeostasis or an ideal state of equilibrium. The sympathetic nervous system (SNS) is very active when we are awake and controls various conscious activities such as the fight-or-flight response. Its activity tends to create wear and tear of the body. Accompanying the SNS, and influencing the same glandular and smooth muscle systems, we have the parasympathetic nervous system (PNS) ruling rest, digestion and sleep.

We have a plant quality in us that builds us constantly—this is an attribute of our etheric vehicle. Working mainly when we are asleep, it is under the governance of the **parasympathetic** nervous system; it favours regeneration and is often called the life force.

Our internal awareness is an inner animation, or movement, which is carried by an astral vehicle. The forces which constitute this awareness have an animal quality, and they consume our plant-like life forces when we are awake. Working mainly when awake, it is governed by the **sympathetic** nervous system; this astral vehicle enables the development of our psychic world by consuming our life forces or the etheric aspect of the growing process in us. Where plants have great sensitivity and ways to respond to their environment (heliotropism), animals have sensorial organs leading to movements through muscular activities. This gives rise to conscious expression of instinctual behaviour—the beginning of soul expression in a physical body.

These two parts of the ANS harmonize the delicate equilibrium between the organ systems. The ANS is separated from our consciousness so that we are not burdened with all the processes which are continually occurring within our bodies—it does not allow us to hear what is going on in the metabolism. If we could we would be dazzled, paralyzed. It would be like walking in a big city with noisy traffic on the road and a building being constructed on one side and another being demolished on the other side.

Layout of the book

A. Introduction: Beyond the static state

Planetary movements
In the womb of pulsed motion
A special alignment of planetary spheres
Rudolf Steiner and the ancient Chinese point of view
Lay out of the book
Lay out of each chapter

B. Seven Chapters

Each chapter explores the impact of one of the Planetary Spheres on our organic make-up (metabolic processes) and psychic activity. The connection between planets and organs is given by Rudolf Steiner in numerous lectures. He considered the living Earth to be nested in a living Solar System that reverberates within us in multiple ways.

The seven chapters will reflect the sensory path of perception inside us. Each will show its forming influences on the psychic life as well as its formative impact on the creation of organ systems. The link between organs and tissues that produce the five specific inner landscapes in relation with the outside rhythmic environment was developed over centuries in Traditional Chinese Medicine.

C. Conclusion

The conclusion of each of the seven sections summarizes the convergence of the subtle and material aspects of the metabolic processes. The soma is made of seven landscapes which reverberate in the psyche, in a healthy or unhealthy way depending upon its condition. The way we use our soma or psyche harmonizes or damages this fragile ensemble. This book enlarges the concept of organs and planets...we can always add further content to our knowledge.

Layout of each chapter

A PREAMBLE accompanies the beginning of each chapter and connects with the whole text. It invites the reader to loosen some conceptions of what reality is and to contemplate new ways of observing. There is an urgency for many scientists to be on the lookout for new paradigms. The simple facts of new observations about the fabric of this world are pushing scientists to reassess their assumptions and working hypotheses. This is how science has always made progress.

Each of the seven chapters is divided this way:

A. One of the seven **stages of life** given by Rudolf Steiner is explored as one of the seven metabolic processes. All seven chapters are a sequence that shows the constant profound impact that the perceptible world has on our psyche as well as our organic make-up.

B. We give an overview of the related Chinese **Treasure organ** with an interpretation of its ideogram and the predominance of a Greek Element. The **Workshop organ** and tissue layer related to this landscape will be touched on briefly by bringing Rudolf Steiner's perspective together with traditional Chinese and modern physiology advantages together.

C. We examine the Chinese ideogram of **the creative spirit** of each set of organ and tissues. Each organ landscape is a function through which the psyche is able to manifest itself. These landscapes that build the body (soma) reverberate as ways for the psyche to operate.

> What makes consciousness possible is not the brain as a producer of consciousness but the processes of the body as a whole. These serve as a mirror reflecting the activity of the soul. The bodily organs as living body processes act as reflectors of psychic activities.
>
> RUDOLF STEINER (9)

> We must know that, in spite of the fact that they are not fully impregnated with conscious life, all the organs contain the source of the surge directing us towards the psychic life.
>
> RUDOLF STEINER (10)

Five primal emotions will be explored briefly (excitement, anxiety, sadness, fear, anger). We will look at the lessons attached to them in order to reach a state of equilibrium between emotional numbness and over-reactivity. We share our primal emotional reactivity with the animals and, through our self-conscious activity, we build with it an aspect of our feeling life. Emotions and feelings expand or contract our organ systems. These internal atmospheric changes impact on the breathing, circulation, the smooth muscles of organs and the glandular system.

D. In his book *The Secrets of Metals*, Croatian chemist, Wilhelm Pelikan (1893 – 1981), coined the term cosmo-biology to emphasize the importance of **metals** continually raining down on Earth from the Cosmos usually as small particles though in vast quantities—NASA estimates about 100 tons per day! Pelikan states that metals are congealed flowing forces. Spectroscopy analysis shows 'metal lights' coming from the Suns of the Universe. A kind of 'metallic signature' in light form rains down on Earth from all over the Universe as well as actual metals in the form of meteors and Cosmic dust. Similarly, the physiology of living beings can't do without metals. We are also continually absorbing quantities of metals through the food we eat. Human history is also intrinsically tied to the materials we learned to exploit with consecutive civilizations—Stone, Bronze and Iron Ages. The old traditions such as Alchemy in Medieval Europe connected each Planetary Sphere with a specific metal.

Metals are everywhere in Nature in states of subtle distribution or mingled with other elements as ores. Some metals are found pure (gold) but most of them are solidly united with other elements (ores). Through the ages of subsequent civilizations, humans have learned to extract and transform metals. Some like bronze and iron could be extracted from the earth relatively simply but others such as aluminium, took a long time to extract because of the need to master electricity to generate enough power to complete the smelting process.

In living creatures metals act not so much as building blocks but as agents energizing physiological activities. They are resonators and oscillators orchestrating the enzymatic activities. Enzymes (which are themselves proteins) are tools that assemble the amino acids to form proteins. They are very sluggish if not accompanied by metals and vitamins as co-factors. Co-factors act at various degrees of dilution where their resonance is in full bloom. Our minute cells can't operate without them and we will try to penetrate their subtle organizing power. Our cells contain tiny amounts of various metals which improve the efficiency of the enzymes.

E. A description of the **Planetary Seal** from a biological perspective. Between 1907 and 1911 Steiner drew the Planetary Seals. They are 'occult scripts' where the lines of each drawing are in dialogue between a centre and a periphery like etheric currents. Each seal has a motif repeated seven times. These seven seals 'mean that within the world of etheric substance, which surrounds us, with all the beings incarnated in it, the forms we see here are actually present [as activities]'. Rudolf Steiner (11)

It is by the study of the activities, and effects of man's bodily fluids and circulation that we shall learn to understand the planetary activities.

RUDOLF STEINER (12)

Many people over the years have meditated on these seals and their contracting/expanding lines that radiate an in-and-out symmetry. Sculptors have experienced the lines of these drawings as the top of convex movements, whereas the space between the lines is more concave. Anthroposophist metalworkers have sometimes carved the seals in the metals assigned to each planet to give them even greater resonance. Creating reliefs out of the form brings us closer to the archetypal activity within. In *The Secrets of Metals*, Pelikan studied a planetary sequence based on the atomic weight of the planetary metals, revealing interesting correlations.

In this book the seals are studied in their mobile succession as metabolic processes. To explain these complex processes Rudolf Steiner invited us towards a specific sequence of bodies in the Solar System where the Sun is still a focal centre point as in the Copernicus system.

Saturn – Jupiter – Mars – Sun – Mercury – Venus – Moon mark each chapter. Following this alignment we are going to see these seals from a biological perspective, animating them from one seal into another. These Planetary Spheres pulse like music around the Earth and resonate in us as metabolic processes with their sets of organs. We won't consider the planets beyond Saturn (Uranus, Neptune and Pluto) because they impact more on the human psyche rather than the activity of our organs.

F. A brief and incomplete **summary of each inner** landscape as found in *Les Cinq Chemins du Clair et De l'Obscur* by Jean-Marc Esyssalet (Trédaniel éditeur).

G. Good basic **dietary and psychic habits** to promote the health of that landscape.

As outside, so inside

This overview comes from *Les Cinq Chemins du Clair et De l'Obscur* by French doctor Jean-Marc Eyssalet in the last few decades and reflects a continuous path of influence between the outer world and our inner world.

1 – Because the Earth on its wobbly axis faces the pole star, we have four sectors of space, north, south, east and west, which have specific properties. However, for our experience of them, these sectors rely on our inhabiting a place on which to stand, which we will call the fifth sector.

2 – The rotation of the Earth (24 hours) with its elliptical movement around the Sun induces five climatic variables.

3 – Through these rhythmic movements of increase and decrease of heat and light, specific transformations are observable. The ancient Chinese split these movements into five HUAs that govern the unfolding of life forms. They reflect the way life appears and passes away.

A. Living creatures, for our ordinary sense experience, start with one cell that contains the **contracted essence** of its development—seed, bud, zygote (WATER HUA).

B. Then the germ **opens** into space through a time process—the unfolding of the first leaves, embryo (WOOD HUA).

C. A period of **full expansion** follows—the rhythmic appearance of leaves, foetus/child development (FIRE HUA).

D. The **possibility of exchange** with the environment through reproduction assuring the continuance of the species—e.g. flowers (aroma, pollen), sexual maturity (EARTH HUA).

E. There comes a period of **drying out** where water or sap withdraw, desiccating the structure—seed maturation, old age (METAL HUA).

4 – The molecular architecture of the plant develops five flavours that can be identified by the mouth and tongue initiating expansion or contraction of the mucus membrane.

5 – Acid, bitter or astringent, sweet, spicy and salty food will extend their effects into the whole body impacting on specific organ systems. The health and stability of organ function and their tissue depend greatly on these flavours. Their contrasting effects on us are readily perceived. Sourness makes us wince and sweet can make us dream away with pleasure. The law of polarity characterizes our internal environment. The heart that brings the blood into full expansion will benefit from bitter substances that contract it. The kidney that brings the blood stream into a state of contraction will benefit from salty substances that expand it. All Chinese dietetic is based on this law of polarity.

6 – The five landscapes of organs generate layers of tissue whose health reverberates back to their organ systems.

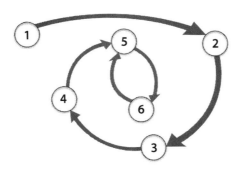

Figure 2: Outside reverberates inside

Each chapter will elaborate on this summary: from the cardinal points outside to inside organs and tissues. (See Illustration 2— Summary) J. M. Eyssalet (13)

A – The observer in the centre of La Rose des Vents
Dampness
HUA—EARTH
Sweet
Spleen landscape—Chapter 1—Saturn Process

B – East
Wind
HUA—WOOD
Acid (lemon)
Liver landscape—Chapters 2 and 3—Jupiter and Mars Process

C – South
Hot
Bitter (coffee)
HUA—FIRE
Heart landscape—Chapter 4—Sun Process

D – West (sunset)
Dryness
HUA —METAL
Spice—(sulphuric food – garlic)
Lung landscape—Chapter 5—Mercury Process

E – North
Cold
HUA—WATER
Salt
Kidney landscape—Chapters 6 and 7—Venus and Moon Process

Note 3: La Rose des Vents (The Wind Compass)

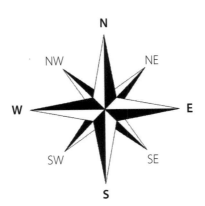

1 – It is from a central point (the fifth sector) in the middle of la rose des vents that the observer experiences the four (sectors) main cardinal points of space.

2 – From this central sector of space, where we are, there is always a level of **dampness**. Water is everywhere even in the middle of the Sahara. From this centre, the observer can perceive four other sectors of space that reveal various aspects of the climate. See Chapter 2—Preamble—Spatial consciousness and climate.

Wherever we stand in the Northern hemisphere, North has a **cold** quality whereas South is **hotter**. East with the sunrise initiates **wind** with its increase of heat, whereas West (sunset) brings **dryness** to the air.

3 – Because of the Earth's rotation and orbit around the Sun we have days, seasons and geological periods that generate constant movements of contraction and expansion in Nature. See Chapter 3—Preamble—A tri-unity in space.

The Chinese created ideograms to show the activity of these recurrent movements of transformation in Nature—they called these the five HUA.

A. East—sunrise, with its increase of heat and light, is WOOD which means a movement of **opening** where the kingdoms of Nature can start to manifest. It is the quality of morning and spring where seed and buds can unfold. It is the childhood of animal species.

B. South—midday brings the FIRE movement, meaning the full **expansion** of the foliage in plants or teenager period in animals.

C. Then a period of maturity called EARTH (the observer— centre of La Rose des Vents) where an **exchange** can occur between the inside and the outside of a living being. It is the budding of flowers releasing pollen, essences, nectar or the period of reproductive capacity of the animals.

D. This is followed by West—sunset with the METAL move- ment, meaning **drainage** (evening or autumn). The water withdraws from the organic structure and the seeds dry out for preservation; for the animal it is old age.

E. With North, the WATER movement, it is night or win- ter in Nature—a **contraction** where Nature is in a resting phase: the dry seeds or buds rest, waiting for Spring to return. There are many variations in this cycle. A tulip can do this cycle in a few months and go dormant for the rest of the year, whereas a carrot takes two years to achieve this cycle. See Preamble Chap. 3—A tri-unity in space.

4 – The impact of this cycle on the plant kingdom creates var- ied molecular architectures that can be grasped consciously with our mouth and our tongue. (See Preamble Chapter 6— Molecular architecture.) Progressively in their development plants produce flavours: acidity (WOOD), bitterness (FIRE), sweetness (EARTH), spices (METAL) and salty substances (WATER). Our internal liquid is composed of many types of salt (minerals) of which NaCl is predominant—the same as common table salt. As food impacts on our mouth these flavours are energy that also contract or expand the function of our organs.

5 – This external cycle reverberates in us and constantly changes the liquid tissues of our body: the blood and lymph. Blood and lymph are the only liquid tissues in the body that connect in their rhythmic flow with all of our organs. Organs in turn have an impact of contraction and expansion on the blood stream.

Each chapter will explore the five main landscapes of organs and tissues (soma) that build up our psychic world.

The spleen (*Saturn*) and pancreas-stomach and duodenum landscape, with its filling tissues shaping the external shape of the body (fat and muscle), is at the centre of all rhythmic **exchanges** between outside and inside, sensorial impressions as well as food (EARTH). It is the beginning of integration of the outside into our internal uniqueness.

The liver (*Jupiter and Mars*)-gall bladder landscape has a constant **opening** Spring effect on the blood stream while its connective tissue establishes the internal territory and its defence (WOOD).

The heart (*Sun*)-small intestine landscape, with its blood and vessels, brings the blood stream to its full **expansion** (FIRE).

The lung (*Mercury*)-large intestine landscape, with its glandular epithelial tissues, coordinates the **drainage** of our liquid (METAL).

The kidney (*Venus and Moon*)-bladder landscape, with its accompanying tissue of bones and marrow (Venus), **contracts** the blood stream (WATER).

References

1 – Rudolf Steiner *The Relation of the Diverse Branches of Natural Science to Astronomy,* Vol. I, Lecture IV, Etheric Dimensions Press, Tobermory, 1999.

2 – Recommended readings: *A Little Book of Coincidence in the Solar System,* John Martineau, Wooden Books. Also *Movements and Rhythms of the Stars,* Joachim Schultz, Floris Books.

3 – See websites on the numerous atmospheric layers and their properties.

4 – Goethe in *Aphorisms on Nature.*

5 – See *The Mystery of Emerging Form,* Yvan Rioux, Temple Lodge, 2017.

6 – See *Occult Physiology* by Rudolf Steiner, Lectures 20 to 28 March, Prague.

7 – Rudolf Steiner in *Forming of Man Through Cosmic Influences*—(*Form, Life, Soul and Spirit*) Dornach, Lectures, 29 October to 5 November, 1921, translated by M. Cotterell.

8 – The ideogram's translations come from Doctor Jean-Marc Eyssalet who, in the last few decades, with a group of Chinese scholars (sinologues) in France, made a translation of the ancient Chinese texts on nature and human physiology, trying to go back to the roots of these compact images. In this text all the ideogram interpretations come from these books. The contents of these books below are as complex as university text books on human physiology. The difference is that the ancient Chinese had more of an eye on the subtle activities of organ systems (landscape) than on isolated organs. They also didn't separate the internal physical organs from their psychic impact. For them body (soma) and soul (psyche) were instruments of a Higher Self (SHEN) in incarnation. They also couldn't separate the external pulse motions of Nature from our inner cosmos of organs.

By Jean-Marc Eyssalet (Guy Trédaniel, Editor):

Les Cinq Chemins du Clair et de l'Obscur.
Shen ou l'Instant Créateur.
Le Secret de la Maison des Ancêtres.
Dans l'Océan des Saveurs, l'Intention du Corps.

9 – Rudolf Steiner in *Psychoanalysis and Spiritual Psychology,* five lectures in Dornach and Munich between 25 February, 1912 and 2 July, 1921.

10 – Rudolf Steiner in *An Occult Physiology,* 1911.

11 – Rudolf Steiner in *Occult Features of the Stuttgart Building,* 15 Oct., 1911.

12 – Rudolf Steiner in *Mystery of the Universe,* Lecture 5 of 16 in Dornach between 9 April and 16 May, 1920.

13 – Jean Marc Eyssalet in *Les Cinq Chemins du Clair et de L'Obscur,* 1996.

CHAPTER 1

SATURN PROCESS
Opening the door of perception
Towards the integration of subtle influences

Preamble: Frequencies versus pulses

All life on Earth is continually bathed in a sea of invisible frequencies, pulses and vibrations. Even sound is simply a mechanical vibration of air or water. Electromagnetic waves consist of oscillating fields in space. These phenomena can be expressed by measuring how often the event repeats itself every second. This measurement is usually calculated using the name of the German physicist, Heinrich Hertz (1857 – 1894) who first conclusively proved the existence of electromagnetic waves.

The seconds hand on a clock moves once every second, this is 1 Hz. The light coming out of a light bulb (in Europe) is 50 Hz, meaning it turns on and off 50 times a second because of the alternating electricity current. The light bulb's light appears continuous because 50 Hz is too fast for our eyes to perceive. But 50 Hz is a very low (slow) frequency compared to some other information signals coming from various radio and microwave frequencies. We have increasing Hz values all through the colour spectrum, X rays, gamma rays and cosmic rays that are calculated by the thousands, millions or even billions of vibrations per second.

Hz is useful to describe an oscillation happening per second but what do we call an event that happens every two seconds, ten seconds or even every eight years like the five loops of Venus (see Illustration 1 in the Introduction) around the Earth seen from a geo-centric point of view? These longer cycles are very common in Nature and within us and we do have a convenient term to describe them: pulsations.

Planetary events are like a choreography and their cycles around us have meaning. All the planets orbiting the Sun are on an elliptical path. This means that sometimes they will be closer to the Earth and sometimes further away as the Earth follows its own elliptical path. These comings and goings of all the planets around the Sun are constant pulsations. On Earth we don't live only in a sea of frequencies but inside a multitude of Nature's own pulsations. Nature nurtures us—what we call Life is in essence rhythmic pulsed motion.

Through *Occult Physiology* it is clear that Steiner considered life as essentially a Rhythm phenomena. Welcome to the realm of the etheric.

This book focuses on pulsations, not frequencies. If we observe some of the complex atmospheric membranes such as the ozone layer of the Earth, we see them constantly approaching and retreating—pulsating... These constant pulsations are neither matter nor energy but they are real and have a material effect. The goal of this book is to describe the pulsing rhythms inside us as well as outside and their connectedness.

Saturn process: opening the door of perception and the beginning of the integration of subtle influences

The spleen, the inner Saturn organ, has in regard to the microcosm man a task similar to the outmost planet Saturn (as far as metabolic processes are concerned), who like a guardian circles around the Solar System and has to change and harmonize with the rhythms of the Solar System all the effects from the zodiac and the rest of the universe. The spleen fulfils for the microcosm man the same task in metabolism. It must equalize all irregularities and foreign rhythms in the substances of nutrition. This activity is carried out by the etheric body of the spleen. The spleen itself may even be removed without detrimental effect upon man.

RUDOLF STEINER (1)

A. Life of the senses—dying life
B. Spleen and its landscape:
   spleen/pancreas—stomach/duodenum,
   tissues
C. Psychic influence: Yi
D. Metal: lead
E. Saturn seal
F. Summary of the spleen landscape
G. For the health of this landscape

A. Life of the senses—dying life

This sense-life is not to be confused with the sense of life (one of the twelve senses according to Steiner) that gives us continual messages (sometimes confusing) from inside related to our wellbeing or sense of pain, thirst, fatigue ...

> The first stage which man in his ordinary consciousness does not generally regard as life, is the life of the senses. The senses are in fact membered into the whole human being, but they lie so much on the periphery that man forgets that the sense-life is the outmost layer of his life. We have the sense-life, however, on the periphery as the outermost layer of our life.
>
> RUDOLF STEINER (2)

In the living world, surface sensitivity is the rule. From a simple bacterial membrane to our own more elaborate skin, these envelopes protect an interiority where an intelligent activity needs a minimum of sensorial input to face the outer world. This is true when we observe the sensitivity of a plant to the Sun (heliotropism of the stem), to gravity (geotropism of the root) and other environmental factors. For instance, the stoma of the leaves of plants can open and close according to wet weather or dry wind. The membranes of all our cells have an array of gluco-lipidic or proteic aerials and alpha-helicoidal proteins making them sensitive to specific substances (such as hormones) and responsive to these signals with a change in their internal metabolism. Like our unique fingerprints, each cell of our body has a marker of their own individuality. These aerials are part of the 'fluid mosaic model' of the membrane. They are important for cell recognition, intercellular adhesion and communication.

The sensitivity/motor activity of the cell membrane is described by the American biologist Bruce Lipton (1944 –) in his book *The Biology of Belief* (16). He is right to consider a cellular membrane as the brain of the cell, and not the nucleus as previously thought. Each living cell in us tastes its environment and reacts to it at its periphery, its 'skin'. Our own brain is like an internal skin which develops in a young child and maintains its activity throughout our lifetime through sensorial input with motor output. Without these stimulations we are more susceptible to dementia because the brain, when not in use, will lose its connective tissue called neuroglia or glial cells (see Note 1 in Chapter 3—Mars).

The Greek Element Water predominates in the liver

In the Animal Kingdom, added to this membrane sensitivity of all the cells, there is also a peripheric sensoriality. This sensoriality is made up of specialist organs designed to decipher certain aspects of the outer world (light, sound, smell, taste, touch) and respond to it.

Facing these external impressions the newborn baby, in its pre-mental stage, is in permanent awe and feels 'at one' with the whole he perceives. He or she wants to grasp this world and taste it. Everything goes into his or her mouth.

The first skin (the ectoderm) of the embryo invaginates (involutes inwards) following the primitive notochord (gastrulation) (see Chapter 5—Mercury Process—Note 1) to produce the neural tube marking the beginning of the central nervous system. Because of this, the sensorial skin will always have an open rapport with the brain. This is why touching and massaging the skin of newborns is actually a precious food for brain development. Touch remains important throughout our lives, not simply as a form of intimacy or human contact but because it is literally 'food' for the brain and has a host of other benefits such as releasing oxytocin and reducing stress levels—our inner world responding to outside stimuli.

Sensorial organs are highly complex apparatuses designed to open us to an aspect of the outer world. Because of this specialization they often lose their capacity to reform or heal if they are damaged; the skin can easily heal cuts or abrasions but damage an eye and that is likely to be permanent. These organic structures (eyes/ears), in order to perceive (light, sound), embody a rigidity and dying process. This dying process, shown in their difficulty to regenerate, is also found in all the neurons carrying impressions to the brain. It seems that in order to consciously receive the outer world we need apparatuses so specialized that they transmute their regenerative powers into a capacity for consciousness to be housed inside an envelope of flesh.

These sensorial inputs provide our consciousness with impressions of the outer world but are also powerful formative inhalations. It is erroneous to think that our conscious perception of light or sound is limited to a specialized sensorial site in the brain. The sense impressions also reverberate inside the body, having an effect on various organs and their metabolic processes. There is a permanent link between our sensory zones and our vital organs. Further chapters will explore this link.

B. Spleen and its landscape

Just below our diaphragm, this breathing muscle that separates the thorax from the abdomen, sits the spleen. It is in an area at the forefront of our inner empire as far as the entry of food is concerned. Any food ingested needs to be transformed. Whether it be vegetable or meat, the food will start to be reduced to its primary organic components in the stomach and duodenum. While the stomach starts dealing with the physical components of the food, what of its more insubstantial qualities, its tastes and its aromas? These have a slightly more nebulous quality and are poorly understood by science and nutrition—they have more to do with chemical reaction and are not energy in a strict sense and yet they can have a huge impact on our inner landscapes. The taste and aroma of all food ingested also needs to be integrated into our unique inner environment. The spleen has a special role to play here.

Spleen

What does traditional Chinese medicine say about the spleen? It is not so much interested in the material organ but more in its activity. The ideogram for the spleen is PI, meaning a cup made of flesh. Here is the image of a container or aerial gathering 'something'—subtle influences. The spleen is a producer of red blood cells in the embryo. After birth it is a graveyard for used red blood cells; red blood cells typically live only three weeks. It is also an etheric vehicle gathering the oscillation of the aromas coming towards us, especially the subtle energies from food and air. These then have to be integrated, made ours.

As the British poet, Walter John de la Mare (1873 – 1956) said in his poem 'Miss T':

It's a very odd thing
As odd can be
That whatever Miss T eats
Turns into Miss T.
[...]

WALTER JOHN DE LE MARE (17)

Taste and aroma are still active beyond the mouth and nose. They easily penetrate the blood stream. If the strong spicy aspect of mustard can impact on the mucus membranes of the mouth and nose, then this spicy essence will carry its chemical reaction and continue its effect inside. An integrative system is in place to receive the multitude of vibratory aromas coming from outside. The etheric aspect of the spleen is at the centre of a complex energetic system of etheric organs (Master of the Heart with the Triple Warmer), the elaboration of which will be studied in the course of later chapters.

As a physical organ the spleen acts on the path of the blood stream just before it enters the liver. On the left side below the diaphragm the blood flows very slowly in a labyrinthine way. The spleen is in the service of the blood stream, digesting red blood cells at the end of their lives, as well as any intruders (bacteria). It is really the servant of the heart/blood stream, as Chinese medicine refers to it. In the embryo, the spleen produces red blood cells in abundance before the cartilaginous skeleton becomes bony with its red marrow.

When we digest, more blood flows to the digestive system. If we eat irregularly while being physically active and thus demanding more blood to the muscles, then the spleen contracts to maintain a good blood supply. An organ full of smooth muscles, it is very useful if we haemorrhage. The contraction of this reservoir of blood can temporarily maintain the right blood pressure. If it contracts too often it inflames and we have to take it out. People can live without a spleen because most of its known functions can be taken over by the liver. Indeed, after passing through the spleen, the blood flows towards the liver.

Steiner in *Occult Physiology* said it is the only organ in our body that will continue to work even if it is removed. What does that mean? He is talking here about functions other than the ones mentioned above. He points out that this organ, in fact, harmonizes the rhythmic entries of the external world with our internal rhythms. So if the physical organ is not there the morphogenetic field, etheric in nature, keeps on working.

'Morphogenetic fields' is a term used by English biologist Rupert Sheldrake (1942 –) to describe how living entities obtain and maintain their shapes, from a tree to a hand to our internal organs. One of the great mysteries of modern Biology is how biological shapes are formed and maintained (18). So far, studying the genes in our DNA has not yielded an answer to this mystery. Rupert Sheldrake postulates that an energy field of morphic resonance must exist for the living tissue to grow into the correct shape and function.

The etheric aspect of the spleen has to do with this 'something' that we inhale rhythmically. The spleen ideogram for the spleen is

PI. Defined earlier as a kind of antenna or cup of flesh, the etheric aspect of the spleen captures the resonating emanations of the external world before being processed internally. Rudolf Steiner had much to say about this:

> The spleen has the task of serving as a sort of regulator of the digestive rhythm.
>
> RUDOLF STEINER (3)

We have seen, for instance, that the seven parts of our universal internal systems [reflection of the seven planetary spheres],—and especially the spleen which is the most spiritual—put a brake in some ways on the external laws that enter with our food [and air].

> This unique microcosm of system of organs acts on these nutritious substances as a kind of filter.
>
> RUDOLF STEINER (4)

All four states of matter (solid, liquid, gas, heat) and their ethers (as symbolized in the Greek Elements) work in the whole organism, but in some major organs one of them prevails.

In the spleen, none of the Greek Elements is predominant. They are equally present in our EARTH landscape where the listening potential (YIN) energy acts equally with the active transformative (YANG) energy. Inside us this EARTH HUA is located below the respiratory diaphragm that separates the thorax-rhythmic organs from the abdomen-metabolic ones. The EARTH ideogram stands for the union and harmony of opposite forces.

Pancreas

The spleen is coupled with the pancreas below the diaphragm. The pancreas' hormones insulin and glucagon are essential in maintaining the fulcrum point of sugar in the blood. Sugar in the blood is the fuel of all metabolic processes and needs to be strictly maintained. Even a slight deviation from the ideal level of concentration of sugar in our blood has a severe impact on us. Too little sugar in our blood (hypoglycaemia) and we become clumsy, confused and will lose consciousness quite quickly. Too much sugar in the blood (hyperglycaemia) can also produce a range of symptoms and is also likely to cause damage to various organs over time. Going into hypo or hyperglycaemia seriously impairs our capacity to use our soul faculties (thinking, feeling, willing). Blood sugar level, like so many other parameters, is maintained through a bio-feedback loop.

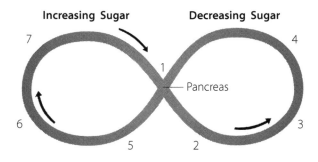

Figure 1: Negative Bio-Feedback Loop Through the Pancreas

Negative bio-feedback

A simple example of a negative feedback loop is the thermostat in our homes. When we set a thermostat at 72 degrees Fahrenheit, we know that the central heating will turn itself off when the thermostat detects that that temperature has been reached. When the temperature drops below the set temperature, the central heating is automatically turned back on. This is a simple but very powerful system. Our body uses various bio-feedback loops where the set point, (the 'temperature' in our example above) is of a specific chemical composition. 99% of hormonal activities are ruled by this system in order to maintain a multitude of fulcrum points that determine health.

In the lemniscate of this drawing (Illustration 1) we have blood circulating and passing through the pancreas (Number 1 in Illustration 1) thousands of times a day. We mentioned earlier that plants have a very refined sensitivity without having sensorial organs as such (eyes and ears, etc....). So it is for cells and organs in our body, they have no sensorial organs as we would recognize them but develop very specific sensitivities. In the pancreas are special regions called Islets of Langerhans which are very sensitive to sugar content in the blood and are important in the metabolism of glucose. In the cycle illustrated above:

1 – In the circulatory system the pancreas is very sensitive to the sugar content of the blood. The normal concentration of sugar (between 70 and 110 mg/dl of sugar in the blood) is mostly determined by this organ. There are other factors such as stress that can change this fulcrum point. As we have seen, we are very sensitive to this point of balance and any variation outside a narrow chemical range will drastically affect our health.

2 – In response to too much sugar in the blood stream such as after a meal, the pancreas (1) responds by releasing insulin in the blood stream.

3 – The cells of the body react by withdrawing sugar from the blood. The liver and fat cells (adipocytes) are especially active here to store the sugar as glycogen and fat.

4 – Through exercises or fasting we decrease the sugar level below the fulcrum point.

5 – Passing through the pancreas (1) again but with a lower sugar level another hormone, glucagon, is released to increase the level of sugar in the blood.

6 – The cells of the body will react by releasing sugar into the blood stream.

7 – This stimulates the increase of sugar in the blood.

And so on and so forth. At the surface of their membrane most cells have 'aerials' sensitive to insulin and glucagon. We can't have a city of organs with their various processes without hormonal modulators that maintain this constant balance.

Of all the planets, it is Mercury that best represents this process of balance. In the glyph for Mercury (Illustration 2) the Sun balances the Moon symbol above (replica) with the Earth symbol below where we come into existence through metabolism. Mercury resonates in us by harmonizing the urge to reproduce with the urge to maintain a balance of substances. Health is a knife-edge experience, constantly in the making.

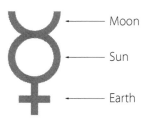

Figure 2: Traditional Glyph for the Planet Mercury

The capacity for the Islets of Langerhans in the pancreas to produce the regulatory hormones for sugar can be compromised by the over-consumption of sugar, especially white refined sugar, because, like salt, it isn't digested but enters the blood stream immediately. This type of refined sugar only became affordable enough to become widespread in European diets during the nineteenth century and its intake as sweets and desserts in the Western world has increased enormously since then. Never before has humankind ingested so much concentrated sugar, starting at a young age, and this bullies the pancreas.

The second function of the pancreas is to provide alkaline juices to the duodenum with enzymes to buffer the stomach acid and facilitate digestion, especially of proteins.

Stomach – Duodenum

These organs are at the frontline of the transformation of food. Humans transform Nature and our environment by taking trees, stones and ores to build houses according to an intention. So it is that we transform the molecular architecture of edible plants and animals into soluble components (amino and fatty acids, glycerine and glucose). As they become soluble they enter the blood stream in order to build a proteic architecture created and sustained by our incarnate spirit.

These workshop organs are also our first line of defence against the microbial world. With its strong acid content, stomach juices neutralize the microbial world. Some of these bacteria and microbes are killed but others are simply immobilized and subsequently become active again where they are more useful, when they enter the large intestine. This acid content also acts as a second 'fragmentar' of organic matter, after the teeth.

The stomach and duodenum preside at the formation of our milky intestinal chyme. We become more autonomous when, in early childhood, we start to produce our own 'milk'. In the ongoing effort to dismantle the outer world (food) we gain a lot of strength. And a multitude of scents, vitamins and micro quantities of minerals will come out of this digestive process and act as energetic activators for the metabolism. Our internal liquids meet the food with litres of high-quality juices ruled by a complex hormonal system of command.

These tubular elastic and muscular organs (stomach and duodenum) have their own grey matter that directs the food from mouth to anus with various peristaltic movements. It is in the duodenum at the sphincter of Oddi that bile and pancreatic juice meet and dilute the food coming from the stomach.

Tissues

Muscles and fat tissue clothe our entire skeleton. When an increase of sugar occurs in the blood stream, the Islets of Langerhans in the pancreas react by releasing insulin to bring down the level of sugar in the blood. This hormone (insulin) mainly activates the adipose cells to make fat, the muscles will store more sugar in their cells and the liver is invited to produce more glycogen (animal starch), the main fuel for the muscles.

Through exercise and food intake we can increase these tissues. Two opposite extremes of this tendency are body building and obesity.

C. Psychic influence: YI

The two quotes below are repeated here from the Introduction because they are crucial to understand if we want to grasp the impact of the soma on the psyche. The five somatic landscapes studied in this book are connected with the spheres of activity of specific organs (heart, spleen, lungs, kidneys and liver). Each of these landscapes provides the psychic basis for the soul to operate.

> What makes consciousness possible is not the brain as a producer of consciousness but the processes of the body as a whole. These serve as a mirror reflecting the activity of the soul. The bodily organs as living body processes act as reflectors of psychic activities.
>
> RUDOLF STEINER (5)

> We must know that, in spite of the fact that they are not fully impregnated with conscious life, all the organs contain the source of the surge directing us towards the psychic life.
>
> RUDOLF STEINER (6)

A psychic capacity resides in each of the five landscapes for the good functioning of our psychic life. The gathering power of the spleen (PI) reverberates at a psychic level. The psychic entity attached to the spleen/pancreas and stomach/duodenum is called YI in Chinese medicine. This ideogram denotes a power to gather thoughts, ideas, insights, memories and deliver them in a coherent way. Is there a better definition of the psychic tool that we call the mind?

When we intend to speak this is a very important gathering tool. If PI (spleen) is essentially a cup of flesh gathering subtle influences from outside, its creative spirit YI is also a gatherer when the intention to speak (heart) emerges in us. It is hard work to stop the mental images. The mind is such a prolific inner cinema. At the same time the YI/mental, as a psychic tool, is always striving to create in our psychic world a coherent picture out of what is perceived. That is how various ideologies emerge—YI is always searching for mental coherence, a middle point of equilibrium (fulcrum) to make sense of what is perceived.

The mind, receiving a primary colour, like yellow, will always produce the complementary one (violet = red and blue) to create an inner equilibrium. YI allows the Spirit to search for coherence.

When we want to recall a happy memory, for instance, the intention starts from the heart area. And then the faithful servant (spleen) will activate a flow of images, sounds and thought forms connected with this event. Sometimes just a smell is enough for this sudden psychic recall. We don't forget anything. It's just that often we don't know how to retrieve it. The creative spirit of the spleen is a gatherer, an aerial, conveying memories to the brain where we become conscious of them.

> The translation (of YI) is 'Imagination'. But we should see here ideation or more the concentration of the mind and the faculty to understand. Children with a deficient spleen don't succeed very well in class. They lack the power of attention. But they can regain it quickly if we can tone up the spleen. Then their understanding of mathematics is much better
>
> GEORGE SOULIÉ DE MORANT (7)

YI (mind) is the psychic instrument that allows the will intention of the creative spirit of the heart to speak. It is the basis of any form of speech—words or gestures. YI is also the understanding of the one who listens to the speech.

Primal emotional reactivity

When we encounter a danger or difficulty in our life, such as losing a job or a partner we lose coherence in our life. Anxiety arises as an over-reflective reaction of the mind that wants to solve a problem and sometimes keeps us from sleeping. This releases stress hormones that make us alert. We share that with the animals when they meet a vital issue in their environment that needs solving.

The presence of this over-reflective state affects the upper abdomen, bringing acidity into the stomach and blocking digestive enzymes from the pancreas. Consequence: impaired digestion.

The lesson of anxiety is always linked to an attempt to re-orient our life goal in search of a new realistic view of oneself.

D. Metal related to Saturn: lead

With our sense organs highly specialized to capture aspects of the outside world, there is a kind of dying and hardening process that works in parallel with organic renewal. That is what lead activity in us is all about: hardening and drying out structures (like specialized senses, nerves and the densification of bones). Our entire skeleton is, like our fingerprint. a dense image of our individuality.

Lead in nature

Lead in nature is naturally peppered all over the Earth, like gold and other metals. Living creatures are all the time exposed to these metals as substance or activity. When the concentration is too high, they have various ways to accumulate them (in the bone structure) or excrete them (through our hair). Our civilization has drastically increased the presence of lead in certain environments with leaded petrol and other industrial functions. As a micro element in us it is not new—it accompanies the natural and constant process of material hardening and dismantlement that occur in us.

> Lead has more natural radioactive varieties (isotopes) than any other element.
>
> WILHELM PELIKAN (8)

The white lead ore, cerussite (lead carbonate), is built of sheaves of needles, it is a network of glittering laminae like a bone structure.

> It is distinguished by beautiful crystal clusters growing in a complex latticework of beams, bars and leaves. These remind us of

the forms in which the fine calcareous traveculae arrange themselves in the heads of bones.

WILHELM PELIKAN (9)

The main lead ore on Earth is lead sulphide (galenite), which
was exploited very early by Europeans. Wilhelm Pelikan, in *The
Secrets of Metals*, states that the Spanish lead mines in the time of
the Roman emperor Titus (39 AD – 81 AD) had more than 50,000
slaves.

Pure lead is like metallic clay—a bad conductor of heat and
electricity at normal temperatures. This is the opposite of silver
which has the highest electrical conductivity of the seven metals
associated with the Planetary Spheres. Lead salt, like lead silicate
(crystal glass) changes light. Whereas silver salt (Moon is our closest
planetary sphere as opposed to Saturn) is changed by light (photo
plates).

The lead ore galenite has a quite gloomy look compared to
other lead ores such as crocoite (red-orange ore—lead chromate)
or wulfenite ore (orange yellow—lead molybdate). These last two
sparkle as though fire itself had fashioned them. The bright colours
betray the fire within. Thus lead unites two very strongly contrasting forces: rigid heaviness and revivifying inner fire. It can
also dissolve gold, just as water dissolves salt.

Lead also has another important quality:

But impermeability to rays of energy such as those given off
by x-rays and radium is a special characteristic of lead and
makes it particularly well-suited to serve as a shield against their
destructive power.

RUDOLF HAUSCHKA (10)

Lead inside us

Lead is more likely to be stored in bones if we have too much
exposure to it. It is a heavy metal and in the human body it is its
vibratory pattern that must act more than the metal. Many other

metals, such as copper, cobalt and others operate in very small quantities as essential enzymatic co-factors in our cells. But not lead. We actually reject lead all the time through our hair or store it in our bone structure.

> Just consider where the strongest forces of decomposition are found in the Earth; where radium occurs we find the strongest forces of decomposition. In lead the cosmos prepares a substance for itself in which to concentrate its most powerful splitting forces. By bringing lead into the human body, you place the body directly amid the processes of world disintegration. [...]
>
> In lead we actually have an effective means of evoking the forces of decomposition.
>
> RUDOLF STEINER (11)

> Lead in minimal doses strengthens the forces of consciousness...
>
> [...] At the same time lead tends, like consciousness, to decrease the regenerative metabolic processes.
>
> WILHELM PELIKAN (12)

The healthy urge to sleep a third of our life is linked with the fact that when we are conscious and using our daily soul faculties we deplete the life forces that renew us.

> On one hand, lead activity helps our body's necessary organic decay in order to renew its structure and, on the other hand, it hardens us by repelling water: without lead there are no crystallized bone structures and no hardened sense organs (eyes, ears, etc.). (13)

Steiner states that the moral stamina of the Romans was greatly compromised over the centuries by the fact that their drinking water was carried by lead pipes. It is interesting to link lead with morality.

E. Saturn seal

The seal has an irradiating centre: is it the beginning of something? The original Solar System at its beginning (Steiner calls it Old Saturn) was just heat, according to Steiner. The Big Bang model is also just heat at the beginning. Amusingly, as the Big Bang model has been refined over the years there is now nothing very big or bang about it. It is an infinitely small point, infinitely dense and hot outside space-time. This point starts to expand (no bang) progressively generating time, space and matter. Heat is always a starting point even if it not strictly speaking a state of matter; it ruled all the other states.

The central lines irradiate into a starry form parting the inner space into two distinct areas. This seven-pointed form modulates the peripheric line creating a succession of concavities and convexities.

On the surface of our face, eyes, ears and skin there are numerous concavities where the senses imbed themselves to capture an aspect of the outer world (light, sound). The first thing that a cell membrane has is sensitivity. Animals and human beings have sensoriality (specialized sense organs). It is the condition of existence for an intelligent interiority to be able to perceive what is outside. Our eyes and ears are formed through living concavities. Even our brain (an inversion of the neural cord) comes from an involuted skin (gastrulation of the ectoderm) in the embryo along the notochord axis. In the case of the eyes, they form out of a move-ment where the brain membrane is going out (inversion of the brain vesicle) meeting the skin moving in (gastrulation of a spe-cific area of the face). (See Chapter 5—Mercury—Figure 3.)

From this description this seal reflects the first life stage: an activity that gastrulates to produce sensorial cavities. Beyond gastrulation (invagination) there is a continuing principle called inversion that we will look at in the Venus seal.

In their attempt to explore the vastness of the Cosmos and the microscopic world of Quantum Physics, scientists are often puzzled. It seems that everything started with infinite heat (hence the Big Bang).

Exploring the origin of the Solar System, Steiner saw simply a state of warmth and called it Old Saturn in his book, *Occult Science*. For him warmth 'is just a finer substance than gas'. Moreover, he said gas itself is none other than 'condensed warmth' or structurally organized particles.

Describing the Old Saturn phase he said it was:

> a different condition from the remaining spatial environment...
> warmer and cooler portions would be alternating with one
> another in the most diverse ways ... irregular figures would be
> arising from the difference of warmth.
>
> RUDOLF STEINER (14)

It is then that:

> the seed-organs are first implanted in the stream of evolution...
> Within the Saturn body something like sensation of taste begins
> to go surging to and fro. Sweet, bitter, sour, etc., are perceived
> at diverse places in the interior of Saturn; while in the heavenly
> space without, all this gives the impression of sound, of a kind
> of music.
>
> RUDOLF STEINER (14)

Were there Beings in the making in that strange heat state?

F. Summary of the spleen landscape [15]

Inner organic world
- Treasure organs: spleen—pancreas
- Workshop organs: stomach—duodenum
- Associated tissues: skeletal muscles and fat tissues (flesh)
- Energy tendency: the YIN (listening + storing energy) balances with the YANG (transformative energy)
- Vitality of the rhythmic exchanges between outside and inside
- Dynamic of the catabolism (bile) and anabolism (fulcrum point of sugar)

At the skin level the inner world perceives, or insures the health of:
- Flavour and texture: the sweet aroma of cooked grains and the flagrance of flowers. The fleshy texture of food
- Body fluid: enzymatic saliva
- Transformed skin: lips—temperature and feel of the food in the mouth

In the psychic world
- Psychic instrument: YI or mind as a coherent gatherer of thoughts and insights. The mind as an instrument that helps the I AM to make ideologies
- Primal emotion: anxiety as an effort to respond to a problem
- Negative feeling: over-concern, worry
- Vocal expression: singing
- The health of a perceptual organ: taste buds of the tongue

G. For the health of this landscape
- The reflective mind is all the time in search of coherence in order to reach a level of equilibrium. Meeting problems in our life leads to anxiety in order to sort out these difficulties. Over-presence of anxiety, worry, over-concern tend to depress this landscape (stomach ulcers).

- Arrange the daily intake of food in a rhythmic way, in a calming convivial atmosphere.
- Reduce the intake of water while eating because it dissolves the essential acidity of the stomach.
- Avoid eating between meals to give a rest to the digestive system.
- Avoid eating while on the move because the blood should flow into the digestive organs rather than the muscles.
- The spleen doesn't like cold food or drink. The liver, the warmest organ, will give its heat to warm it up, but the spleen will suffer more and tighten its smooth muscles.
- Deal with dampness in the house—it fosters fungus and mould.
- Avoid white sugar or too much sugar—it bullies the pancreas.
- Keep the mindset (ideology) mobile: no dogma.

References

1 – Rudolf Steiner, *Forming of Man Through Cosmic Influences, (Form, Life, Soul, Spirit),* 28 October – 5 November, 1921, Dornach (translated by M. Cotterell).

2 – Idem.

3 – Rudolf Steiner in a discussion with the workers building the Goetheanum 5 January, 1923.

4 – Rudolf Steiner in *Occult Physiology,* Lecture 7, 27 March, 1911.

5 – Rudolf Steiner in *Psychoanalysis and Spiritual Psychology,* 25 February, 1912 – 2 July 1921, Dornach and Munich.

6 – Rudolf Steiner in *Occult Physiology.*

7 – George Soulié de Morant in *L'Acupuncture Chinoise.*

8 – Wilhelm Pelikan in *The Secrets of Metals.*

9 – Idem.

10 – Rudolf Hauschka in *The Nature of Substance.*

11 – Idem—quote by Steiner.

12 – W. Pelikan in *The Secrets of Metals.*

13 – Idem.

14 – Rudolf Steiner in *Occult Science.*

15 – Jean-Marc Eyssalet in *Les Cinq Chemins du Clair et de l'Obscur,* Trédaniel.

16 – *Biology of Belief*—Bruce Lipton.

17 – Walter John de la Mare—poem: *Miss T.*

18 – 'The shape of life: Biology's biggest mystery', *New Scientist,* 29 August 2012, Roberta Kwok.

CHAPTER 2

JUPITER PROCESS

Preservation of outer perceptions
Establishment and defence of the territory (immunity)

Preamble:
Our spatial consciousness and outer climate

Wherever we stand on Earth there are always four main horizontal directions that we are aware of (North, East, South and West). These cardinal points have connections with the forces of the dense world ever present around us. If we face East to the sunrise we observe in its daily and seasonal rhythms, a return to light and heat, an opening of possibility. These are morning or spring qualities where life can start or continue to unfold whereas in the West, with the sunset, light and heat decrease. These are evening or autumn qualities verging towards contraction.

Note that when we refer to North and South in this context we are referring to a northern hemisphere point of view—this is where the experience of the European and Chinese viewpoints come from.

When sunrise (East) increases heat, the air will rise when it becomes warmer allowing colder air to replace it—Sunrise and East are therefore also associated with *wind*. At sunset (West) the decrease in heat provokes *dryness*. Cold air can't retain as much water as hot air—dew forms on the grass and condensation appears on our windows.

The Sun is lower in the East/West axis in the winter and higher in the summer. The whole of Nature is influenced by this. If we face East, our front and back stand aligned with the electric field of the Earth whereas the North/South axis, to our left and right, is in line with the magnetic field of the Earth.

The north space of a house, because it has less light and heat, is *colder* and has a contracting effect. Nevertheless the cold wind from the North is always refreshing with less water and dust in it, especially after a storm and charged with a pranic vitality (negative ions).

The South, on the other hand, has a more expansive quality, *heat*. The south wind has more fertilizing dust and water in it. We can see how these sectors of space impact on the climate. Of course in the southern hemisphere the situation is reversed. Their South, source of cold, is like our North and the seasons are reversed.

In the first four years of life, we master the art of walking. Moving in an upright position, we become more acutely aware of gravity and the up/down direction. These three directions of space (front/back—left/right—up/down) are the ones we are most aware of.

In our awareness of the four cardinal points or sectors of space we always stand in the crossing point of La Rose des Vents (the fifth sector). In there we always experience a certain level of *dampness* because water moistens everything. (See La Rose des Vents at the end of the Introduction.)

Nevertheless, space as such is not limited to these directions in three dimensional space. Supersensible formative influences, carried by the light of the stars and their rays of frequencies of all kinds, come towards us from infinite directions of space and sustain us all the time. Each time we breathe in, our skin and lungs are under these climatic and cosmic influences.

Because of our bi-lateral symmetry, human beings have a conscious perception of these space directions. What kind of consciousness is there in a creature like a starfish with its pentaradial symmetry? Living in water it perceives very little gravity and only the up-down direction of space. Turn a starfish upside down and it becomes acrobatic in an attempt to return to the right up-down position. Because its 'eyes' are at the ends of its five extremities, there must be no experience of left/right or front/behind in such a conscious creature.

We are human because we must continually create a state of balance between above and below, forward and back, and left and right.

RUDOLF STEINER (1)

The Earth's movement around the Sun, in an eccentric circle, and the Earth's rotation around its own axis are the first and second law of Copernicus's system.

Copernicus's third law is:

about the Earth's movement around the Sun in relationship to the seasons and precession. As astronomy progressed, it failed to consider this third Copernican law in its entirety. In fact, Copernicus's successors effectively eliminated it.

RUDOLF STEINER (2)

We need to reinstate it, and a good approach would be to plunge into an understanding of the five Chinese movements (HUA) where Humankind is the central point of convergence. These movements of transformation accompany the unfolding of the living kingdoms with their pulsations. The ancient Greek civilization too, made similar observations concerning the qualities of these sectors of space.

Jupiter Process—The preservation of outer perception and the establishment and defence of an inner territory (immunity)

A. Life of the nerves—preserving sensation
B. Liver and its ideogram
    its landscape (liver—gall bladder)
    nourishing the connective tissues
C. Psychic influence: HUN
D. Metal: tin
E. Jupiter seal
F. Summary of the liver landscape
G. For the health of this landscape

A. Life of the nerves – preserving sensation

> We have the sense life [Saturn Process]...on the periphery as the outermost layer of our life [to perceive the outer world]. If we go further towards the interior, we come to the nerve-life that is the life of the senses continued inwards. The nerves as we know proceed inwards from the sense organs.
>
> RUDOLF STEINER (3)

What is a brain if not a very complex matrix of interconnected nerves carrying streams of nervous influxes with, in its centre, two master glands (hypothalamus/hypophysis and pineal) that bring a vital coherent hormonal balance to the rest of the body.

We need nerves to preserve sensation. The first four years of life are extremely brain formative. It is well known that sensorial deprivation in the early years has a detrimental effect on our future conscious perception. The rule is simple: use the nerve or lose it. Operating on the eyes of a person blind from birth doesn't give full perception.

The eyes of a newborn don't see as we do. Receiving the interplay of light and shadow, the consciousness of the baby tries to decipher more of this strange moving phenomenon and develop the occipital area of vision in the brain. So here we have an inner Presence that wants to explore what is coming from outside through the eyes. It is in this dialogue that cells (oligodendrocytes and Schwann cells) surrounding the axon of the nerve, coil more layers of phospholipids essential for the efficiency of the nerve activity (nervous influx).

Only the stimulation of the nerves in early childhood will induce the oligodendrocytes and Schwann cells to curl more and more around the neuronal prolongations (axons) providing more phospholipid sheaths facilitating the vital bio-electric current (nervous influx). Their formation occurs mainly in childhood through sensorial and motor activity.

(See Note 1 in the Mars Process—Chap. 3 about the neuroglia or connective tissue of the brain.)

Sensorial impressions, including touch, are real food not just for developing our senses but also in the sculpting of the brain.

The spinal cord/brain is an involuted skin that appears right at the beginning in the embryo. No random activity here but a strange choreography showing a will to interconnect a sensory input with muscles output. That is what a baby does: senses the world and experiences its muscles by grabbing it.

The brain, as an inner skin, re-constructs all the time. Even at 72 years it is still possible for new neurons to be formed in the frontal lobe (4). There is however, a condition: we have to be mad about life, in an enthusiastic frame of mind without rigid pre-conceptions or ideologies. The brain, like many other organs will atrophy if it is not used. The lack of sensory and motor activity in the elderly has to be addressed in connection with dementia. The brain is, in essence, formed and healthily maintained through sense perceptions and motor activities. Reduce these activities and the neuroglial cells collapse. They reproduce if the sensorial and motor aspect of the brain is active. We must find ways to keep the brain active and challenged through physical activity, crosswords, hobbies, card games, puzzles, chess etc…

As adults we have ten times more neuroglial cells than neurons. These nursing cells can reproduce as long as there is neuron stimulation. Without it the astrocytes (the cells of the neuroglia) that build the scaffolding between blood vessels and neurons, shrink and the brain can't operate; it collapses and the brain-blood barrier becomes permeable to toxins.

In all the billions of nerve cells that carry nervous influx (bio-electricity) not one neuron touches another. There is always a tiny gap (synapse) between them. The transfer of the influx is done by a neurotransmitter such as acetylcholine. Interestingly, these neuro-transmitters can sometimes act like hormones and hormones, such as secretin produced by the stomach, can act on the neurotransmission.

Deprivation of sensorial and motor activity in early childhood is detrimental to the child's future brain growth. If a child doesn't hear language in the first few years of its life, the relevant centres in the brain don't develop and the child won't be able to speak. So it is for many aspects of brain development stimulated by sense impressions.

The way the nervous system relates with the endocrine and immune system is also settled in these first four years and is called the primal adaptive system.

Three essential things are learned in our first four years of life:

'The **First** is the equilibrium of his own body in space'—standing up against gravity and walking

Second, learning 'to talk, when his soul's inner being i.e., that which is carried on from one life to another, is stimulated. The germ, for the development of the larynx must be formed during the period at which the embryo has not yet acquired his ego-con-sciousness' (pre-mental state)

Third; ' the life within the world of thought itself. The elaboration of the brain happens because the brain is the instrument of thought. At the beginning of life, this organ is still plastic, because the individual has to form it for himself as instrument of thought, in accordance with the intention of the entity which proceeds from one incarnation to another...he must remodel the inherited peculiarities of his brain.'

RUDOLF STEINER (5)

Four years to learn all this—it's like getting an undergraduate degree!

B. Liver and its landscape

The Chinese ideogram for liver is GAN—a pestle of flesh meaning an active gesture that **dismantles** and **transforms**. It also means a **shield**.

If we look at the blood flow in the human body, it is the liver that is the main provider of heat for the brain and nervous system at night. During the day, our active muscles also produce heat as we move. Without heat the nerve cells become numb. Frozen fingers in the winter are insensitive. Cold-blooded animals such as reptiles are immobilized by cold.

The liver is the warmest organ, soft and spongy, with a kind of plant-like capacity to regenerate if cut. Located just beneath the diaphragm (on the right side), the liver acts as a biochemistry lab juggling with organic matter. Its capacity to transform sugar, protein and fat into one another is proverbial. Its polyhedra microstructures remind us of a frantic beehive. Receiving the flow of digested nutrients from outside, the liver is the first organ to remodel the dismantled organic world (food). The blood coming out of the liver experiences a spring effect. The portal vein entering the liver carries the blue blood from all digestive organs and the spleen and the gall bladder. It is fed oxygen by arterioles (red blood) connecting with venules (blue blood) just before the large capillaries (sinusoids). This is quite a unique set-up.

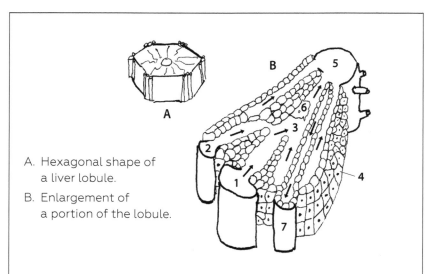

A. Hexagonal shape of a liver lobule.

B. Enlargement of a portion of the lobule.

Figure 1: Hexagonal liver lobules

1 – A hepatic portal venule (small blood vessel) enters the liver lobule charged with the new substances from the digestive organs, the gall bladder and the spleen. This blood lacks oxygen. Being rich in carbon dioxide (CO_2), we call it blue blood.

2 – An arteriole (small artery) of the hepatic artery rich in oxygen mingles with the blue blood before entering (3) an enlarged capillary (sinusoid). In the body, it is rare for an arteriole to meet a venule before a capillary bed.

4 – The liver cells (hepatocytes) start to work on this blood stream. These cells perform a vital task by cleansing the blood and producing new substances (see the liver function section B). The sinusoid circulation goes towards a branch of the hepatic vein in the centre of the hexagon (5) and will connect with the vena cava on its way to the heart.

6 – Huge macrophages (Kupffer cells) are present in the sinusoids digesting any intruders or dead red blood cells.

7 – In all this complex activity the hepatocytes have time to excrete a liquid bile that a branch of the bile duct carries to the gall bladder for concentration. This bile is an essential component of the digestive process (see Mars Process, Chapter 3). Millions of these hexagonal lobules work frantically like bees in a hive to transform the blood with new substances. The liver has a 'spring effect' opening the blood to new possibilities.

The liver opens the blood to constant renewal. It has a spring effect on the blood: it is the WOOD movement. Its ideogram means pull and push in a vertical spiral in the plant (germination). In us it stimulates the establishment and defence of our territory.

Completely new substances are created, like glycogen (animal starch) for movement and thermoregulation. Glycogen production follows a circadian (daily) rhythm with a maximum accumulation in the liver during the day and a maximum excretion in the blood stream at night.

The liver is also the ruler of cholesterol, an integral part of all cellular membranes and the starting point for the construction of steroid fatty hormones (testosterone, oestrogen) as a basis for sexual identity. Cholesterol is also involved in myelin sheath production around the neurons essential for the efficiency of the transmission of nervous influx.

Additionally, the liver produces the proteins that carry the fatty steroid hormones in the blood stream and a huge amount of other proteins for scarring and the immune system. It can store minerals and vitamins as well as toxic substances.

The liver cells (hepatocytes) also produce the bile which is an essential component for digestion and assimilation of the milky chyme in the small intestine. (See Mars—Chapter 3—gall bladder.)

The Greek Element Water predominates in the liver

> Therefore, in studying the activity of the organs we come into contact with the world of the Elements.
>
> RUDOLF STEINER (6)

The ancient Greeks knew about an etheric presence accompanying a state of matter. Steiner elaborated more on this subject in many lectures such as *Occult Physiology*. An etheric presence means an intelligent activity that has a role in Nature's transformation. In *Les Forces de Vie* (1981), Victor Bott, Paul Coroze and Ernst Marti describe these etheric Elemental forces that are not the same as the formative ones.

In the liver, the chemical/sound ether, linked with the liquid state of water, is the most active. The chemical elements and organic substances are related by corresponding octaves of reactivity from zero reaction (for the inert gases) to +1, +2, +3, +4, -3, -2, -1 etc... It is all about the capacity for substances to be a donor or a captor of electrons. Around 1926, American natural philosopher Walter Russell wrote *The Universal One* in which he organizes the young Periodic Table into octaves of reactivity. Following his train of thought he was able to predict unknown elements that later completed the Table. Sound and music also operate with various octaves. Sound is considered an ether because, like the other ethers, it has a quality that keeps matter in movement. It is an organizing force (see Chladni plate demonstration on YouTube).

Ether and state of matter are in polarity. Steiner stipulates that the ethers are peripheric whereas the states of matter are more central.

Liquid state: spherical drops that fuse with one another to form a continuum. The solid state keeps its mass but loses weight when within the liquid state. The liquid state allows fusion (fecundity). It is compact and gathers drops into a flowing stream.

Chemical or sound or music ether: a quantity made of discrete parts that separate, as in cell division governed by a centriole (nine triplets of tubular protein). It is well known that tubular structures are resonators. The African tam-tam is a hollowed tree, the sound of which can travel long distances. The sound fragments, is porous and divides.

The Earth turns on itself as well as orbiting the Sun while pulsing (daily tidal waves). The same thing with faster movements happens to electrons around a nucleus in all atoms. A child's Victorian top, when spun, makes a sound and has an erratic wobble. It is an interesting metaphor for the behaviour of ultra-small objects. Atoms are known to be harmonic oscillators. Harmonic musical principles play an essential part in our bio-chemistry. With ever more powerful microphones we are beginning to be able to listen to chemical reactions. We might discover that blood and sap are marching sounds and each organ has its own sonic field.

Nothing is static in this physical world; everything is an interactive multitude of vibratory waves. All objects radiate sound waves, emitting formative sonic fields. In his *Harmonices Mundi* (1619), German mathematician Johannes Kepler's (1571 – 1630) third law stipulated that the whole Universe—atoms and galaxies—are ruled by this same law of the mutual dependence of bodies freely moving in space. The ancients called it the Music of the Spheres.

We must clearly understand that the liver also possesses an etheric organ; it is this later which, in the first place, has to do with music...for the liver is very closely connected with all that may be summed up as musical conceptions that live and resound in man.

RUDOLF STEINER (7)

All chemistry outside or inside us works with the same laws of numbers or music or octave of reactivity.

The liver has not only a watery consistency but it also regulates [water of the whole] body's household which is a comprehensive task since two-thirds of our body consist of fluids.

RUDOLF STEINER (8)

Which makes water intake the main food for the liver.

Gall bladder
See Chapter 3—Mars Process

Connective tissue
Like the three layers of connective tissues in the muscles (Figure 2) the nerves also have three sets of envelopes. Every single nerve fibre is surrounded by a crystalline perineural system.

1 – Elongated skeletal muscle cells and nerve axons are wrapped in a layer of connective tissue (endomysium for muscle cells and endoneurium for axons).

2 – The muscle cells and axons are bundled up into another layer (perimysium for muscle cells and perineurium for the axons).

3 – The whole muscle and nerve have an external covering (epimysium for the muscle and epineurium for the nerve).

4 – A muscular fibre or an nerve axon. When the three wrapping layers of a muscle meet at the end they fuse and form a tendon that becomes bone. When the fibrocytes of the

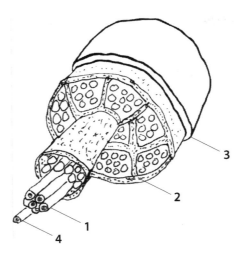

Figure 2: Muscle and Nerve Coverings
(See Note 3—summary of the connective tissue.)

connective tissue reach the bone they change into osteocytes for bone construction. The ligaments attach bone to
bone; the tendons attach muscle to bone. Because the skeletal muscle cells don't touch one another, each one receives
a nerve ending in order to contract. Blood vessels and nerves
are not present in this drawing. The main properties of muscles are excitability bringing contraction and movement.
They can stretch and are elastic.

Whereas the neuron cells operate in a classical digital way (that
is to say either nervous influx or no nervous influx), these layers
works on direct semi-conduction current.

'Because these envelopes can carry information, R. O. Becker
states that it is a distinct communication system.' (9) The distinction between sensorial and motor nerves becomes blurred.

A motor nerve carries a bio-electric current from the brain to a
muscle, but the envelope of that nerve has the possibility, through
semi-conduction, to carry information back to the brain. In fact
every nucleus of a cell connects with this matrix and is in tension

with it, is integrated with it. This confirms Steiner's suggestion that there is no such thing, strictly speaking, as a sensorial or a motor nerve, each nerve has both functions. This drastically changes our understanding of how the body operates. We are on the verge of a completely different understanding of human physiology. Two currents flow: a motor or sensorial nervous influx (bio-electricity) carried by the axons of the nerves and another stream of information carried by the semi-conduction property of its connective tissues (perimesium). There is also a constant communication between the nerve ending (cell extensions like axons) and its cell body or grey matter where the nucleus resides. (See Note 1 on axonal transport.)

Note 1—Axonal transport

Between a nerve cell and its axon extremities, there can be a metre's distance—e.g. the sciatic nerve. Some organelles and proteins, such as neurotransmitters, need to be carried in the axon. An helicoidal network of micro-tubes, made of tubulin proteins, provides the main cytoskeletal 'track' for transportation in the axons.

If we want to understand the **shield** effect in the liver ideogram GAN we need to penetrate the nature of the connective tissue, the vitality of which depends on the liver according to Chinese medicine. In the symbol of a shield there is a 'domain' to protect. Observation shows us that any living unit, be it a cell with its membrane or human beings with their skin, needs an enclosure to manifest its project. Because each organ in us has a specific function in regard to the blood stream it has to be isolated. This is a biological law arising out of a simple observation. That is why organs (volumes) have protective shields (surface membrane) in which they dwell, whether the pericardium for the heart or the red muscle wrapping of each individual cell. These shields are made of connective tissue. They separate, envelop (serous membrane, meninges), attach (ligament, tendon) and unite everything. Internal sensoriality resides in this tissue where the blood capillaries communicate with cells and where the defence and inner digestive system starts. From nerves to blood vessels to organs, everything is wrapped in this protein-liquid-crystal watery tissue.

We know that the solid state of the mineral kingdom is crystalline. We also now know that 'Crystalline arrangements are the rule and not the exception in living systems.' (10) Physicists know a great deal about the properties of crystals. For example, certain kinds of crystals are piezoelectric (quartz)—that is, they generate electricity if they are compressed or stretched. Furthermore, it has been shown that 'Virtually all the [connective] tissues in the body generate electric fields when they are compressed or stretched.' (11)

Bones are living solid crystals constantly emitting piezo (see Note 2) signals when in use (compressed or twisted). This favours greatly the constant rebuilding of the bone by the osteocytes that are constantly producing a matrix of calcium phosphate and collagen. It is well known that electric fields are used to accelerate the healing of injured bones in sport injuries. Astronauts living in low gravity lack the compression of the bone structure and their bones lose density. This is easy to repair through exercises when they come back to Earth and its gravity. It has been demonstrated that weight-bearing activity with people suffering from osteoporosis increases the bone density, along with the right intake of nutrients (calcium and vitamin D).

Note 2—Piezoelectricity

It is a property of crystalloid material discovered in 1880 by Pierre and Jacques Curie. Piezoelectricity is a response to applied mechanical stress such as pressure to a crystal (quartz, bones, various crystalloid protein constructions and even DNA helicoidal proteins). An oscillating electric current is generated called piezo. Crystal materials are made of layers or lattices and applied stress increases friction between the layers that awakes electron activity. It is a quantum phenomenon where some quanta of energy (electrons in this case) start to oscillate and move when compressed or stretched.

Connective tissue also has a crystalloid structure. All of its protein fibres are helicoidal and are organized in lattices. (See Note 3 on the connective tissues.)

Note 3—Connective tissue overview

Connective tissue is essentially a system of envelopes (fascias) and ropes where the organs can nest to perform their metabolic functions. It separates and isolates everything. Each organ has its envelope, such as the peritoneum for the digestive system or pleura for the lungs.

The connective tissue also unites everything. All our organs are suspended to the bone frame with ligaments.

It is in this tissue that the blood flows reaching every cell at a capillary level. This is where the lymphatic system starts.

Our inner sensoriality, informing the brain about our inner environment, is in this tissue.

Having no blood vessels, the epithelium and cartilage depend on connective tissue for nourishment.

Through its fibres it allows compression (collagen) and elasticity (elastin) throughout the body.

Because of its highly crystalloid fibre make-up with structured water, it has semi-conduction properties that convey signals of all kinds (bio-photons, subtle sounds, electron transfer).

It is in this tissue that the battle takes place against invaders and the repair of wounds occurs.

It is the best candidate through which the etheric liquid light of the meridians can travel.

The whole thing swims in 'structured' water. A liquid water molecule is one of those rare substances that has a positive and negative pole at the same time. This allows the simple molecules of H2O to hold hands (weak bond) together forming strings, surfaces and volumes. According to its own movement and mineral content, its structure changes all the time. If water is still, its macro-structure is more stable. But as soon as water flows the bonding of molecules is on the move. Our internal tissues are bathed in water at a quasi mono-layer level.

Surrounding the dense helicoidal proteins of the connective tissue, this mono-layered water has more of a structured stability acquiring crystalline properties. It is difficult in a lab to access this structure because it is all the time on the move as soon as we interfere with it.

> The structure of liquid water is debated, and it is suggested that in biological systems some may have three-dimensional structure.
>
> J. L. OSCHMAN (12)

Scientists have more and more interest in studying the properties of matter at a mono-layered level. Graphene, as a mono-layered carbon is one such recent example.

The protein fibres are omni-present inside and outside the cell and are linked together. This living matrix continuum links the nucleus of every cell with its surrounding. Any tension or pressure on these connecting membranes moves the lattices of this living crystalline tissue and generates bio-electronic signals that can travel in the matrix. Having semi-conductive properties, the connective tissue (made of protein fibres such as collagen, elastin, tubulin ...) can carry signals of all kinds, be it a photon, a sound or a piezo signal which means that the brain, and all cells in this respect have a 'sub-conscious' access to everything that happens in every corner of our inner territory at any time.

The outside world is not only full of sound but also pulsed electro-magnetic radiations coming from the cosmos. Our techno-civilization has increased these background radiations by orders of magnitude in the range of radio and micro wave frequencies for the purposes of communication. Several studies are starting to ring the alarm bell against the intensity of this exposure and the long-term detrimental effect on biological systems. After all, our internal environment is a subtle coherent system immersed in a greater world.

Being highly sensorial, the connective tissue is the perfect candidate to carry the etheric liquid light in these elusive meridian channels shown in Chinese physiology books. This subtle liquid light is not to be confused with the strange phenomenon of bio-photon emission where a particle (a quantum of energy) is on the move. German bio-physicist Fritz-Albert Popp (1938 –) and others observed that living tissues can produce and transmit bio-photons. These bio-photons are coherent light (like a laser). (13) What effect do they have on the whole? In this area of research, we are again on the brink of a completely new understanding of human physiology. What we have inside our little world like in the greater world is an unbroken wholeness and part of what is going on is triggered by 'quantum fluctuations'. (14)

A computer is not an exact analogy to explain our inner communication system. Both, of course, work with mysterious properties of matter. It often happens in the realm of inventions that we just copy what is already active in nature (e.g. the creation of paper by wasps). It seems that we can't invent anything but only discover the mysterious properties of what is already there. Technology is based on this, and in the last few centuries we have increased enormously our technical creativity. What was science fiction yesterday (Jules Verne) is reality today. And this techno-creativity seems to come faster and faster catapulting the future into the present.

The technology we have, based on the forces of electricity and magnetism, is the shadow aspect of the supersensible or flow of formative forces from the constellations and planets informing matter into various kingdoms. The pulsing liquid light of the meridian impacts on all bio-chemical processes generating electricity and magnetism.

Sensitive apparatus capturing the electric potential of the skin can identify the acupuncture points of the skin meridians. This doesn't mean that we are merely a complex electrical machine. This liquid light flowing in our meridians with a circadian rhythm is part of the anatomy of the etheric body and comes from the mingling of the subtle influences of the external world (food, air) and our own father-mother genetic heredity.

Immune system

Our inner territory needs a defence system. There are two aspects at work here, an inner cleansing system and a protection against outside invaders. The first aspect is our inner cleansing system. Cells die all the time and need to be digested. We saw in the Saturn Process the digestion of red blood cells in the spleen. Like our fingerprint, each cell has a marker of our individuality (loose aerials on the surface of their membranes). Getting old they lose the marker. The white blood cells don't recognize them and gobble them up. No healing of wounds happens without white blood cells and they are numerous.

The other aspect of the immune system protects the territory against invasion. Nature around us has its own digestive system. These are bacteria spread everywhere that transform everything, even rock. Bacteria have been found that can digest and transform virtually any substance on Earth, even plastics. Encouraging researches to find primitive organisms such as Ideonella sakaiensis that can digest plastic are on their way. Bacteria are Fermentors and are in symbiotic association with every living creature. But they have to be kept at bay at the periphery of our body (which includes the inner skin of the lungs, digestive and urinary systems). At this boundary multiple defence lymphatic ganglions and bio-chemical tools (antibodies) are present to identify any intruders and digest them.

The liver provides some basic substances (coagulating and immune agents) that help the white blood cells in their defence and repair of the territory. Not surprisingly, in Chinese medicine, the liver is called the General of the Army or the Guardian of the inner territory. The lymphatic ganglions provide other antibodies against specific intruders (bacteria) or substances unknown to the body, such as pollen.

C. Psychic influence: HUN

What kind of psychic entity or surge is coming from this liver/gall bladder area directing us towards the psychic life? We already observed a set of organs/tissue that rule the establishment of a territory and is equipped to defend it. This will reverberate in our psyche.

> The liver…is pre-eminently the organ that gives the human being the courage to transform a deed which has been thought of into an accomplished deed…the liver is the mediator which enables an idea that has been resolved, to be transformed into an action carried out by the limbs [will-metabolic process].
>
> WALTER HOLTZAPPEL (15)

What is the creative spirit of this body landscape (liver, gall bladder, connective tissue, etc) giving us a tool of expression for our soul faculty?

In Chinese medicine it is called HUN. The ideogram HUN has the radical GUI that represents subtle elemental beings building that landscape, with its own thirst for life, often assertive in the outer world. The ancient Greeks were also aware of these subtle 'genies' or natural psychic forces (the Elementals in Nature). They are the builders of the natural world and are 'enchanted' in our various inner states of matter. The other root of this ideogram (HUN) is YUN—a cloud coming out of the mouth meaning the power to speak.

HUN is made of urges for survival with regard to food, shelter and territory. This drive allows a minimum of control over the physical world. In HUN there is a will in the species to affirm itself, as well as an urge to make things (crafts), to survive with the raw material of the environment. It is the power of the warrior; power as a drive of any living creature to actualize its project.

With HUN we have this psychic orientation to transform the external world.

GUI and YUN reflect the formative power of personality through the words we speak and also the potential to transform the outer world according to our physical and psychic needs. It is the realm of the metabolic intelligence—a bursting will-force of movement towards the outside for expression and survival.

The GUI or elemental being in us re-construct our body all the time but can manifest their presence as a polymorphous web of insatiable desires orienting our psyche towards more and more material things, control, and sex. There is something greedy about these GUIs, creating an insatiable need for possessions and control in our will metabolic force.

Primal emotional reactivity

The emotional reactivity related to HUN is anger. What is anger in animals? This emotion arises when a known factor endangers the physical territory or the young of that species. Animals are very territorial, especially at the time of reproduction and that basic reaction helps them defend their vital space. The defence/control of a territory is a vital positive aspect of anger. This is exactly what the liver landscape is doing in our body (soma).

For human beings there is no self-realization without HUN, be it a shelter for a family or a territory for a nation. This extends to a psychic territory essential for any creative process, so anger is the basic energy that allows the creation, defence and expansion of physical or psychic territory. In its hyperactivity or volcanic aspect, anger can become constant irascibility, 'control-freak' behaviour and rage. In its hypo-activity, through self-blame or guilt, we can't create our own space to realize our project. These extremes of distorted feelings occur mainly in human beings.

Anger is warrior energy for self-germination of the talents we are born with. Anger gives us stamina to create our own space in this world and directs the blood flow towards expansion and the power to act. Hyperactivity of this energy can bring too much bile into the duodenum when no food is present (leading to ulcers).

Hypo-activity can lead to a densification of bile in the gall bladder (leading to gall stones). In many cultures the first condition tends to affect men and the second women, because in a patriarchal society men are given more permission to assert themselves—women are conditioned to be nice and obey.

The lesson of anger is self-assertion.

D. Metal related to Jupiter: tin

An understanding of its properties can give a clue to Jupiter's activity in living creatures as an element.

Tin in nature

Tin is not very abundant as a mineral and the only important ore is cassiterite. Bronze is an alloy of copper and tin. Tin seems to have an aversion to water and its ore is completely dry. It tends to repel water. On long exposure to freezing temperatures, it disintegrates to dust.

Tin inside us

If we look at various organs of cattle, the tongue mucosa, as well as muscle and skin, have the largest amount of tin (between 6 and 26 mg. per kg live weight). As far as soft internal organs are concerned, the liver has the most tin (2.14 and 3.73 mg per kg live weight). (16)

Tin's function in living tissues is not well understood and seems to relate with the right proportion of water at the right place. Tin brings plasticity and rigidity into harmony and a correct relation between liquid and solid.

> Tin builds dams to keep water in its place, as it does for example in the brain. Hydrocephalus is an illness caused by tin deficiency, and is often accompanied by a too soft condition of the bones. In speaking of tin we do not, of course, mean the substance, but its formative forces [acting as a co-factor of enzymatic activities].
>
> R. HAUSCHKA (17)

In the construction of our body, in infancy, a balance of forces must be struck between solid bones and softer parts and that, 'the same forces are active in this as in tin' (18).

Tin harbours a cosmic force that draws plastic forms out of fluids.

R. HAUSCHKA (19)

Tin is also used as a solder. What is a soldering process but a joining of two pieces of metal with the help of tin?

R. HAUSCHKA (20)

In the joints we discover a metamorphosis of the forces that produce a proper relation between the solid and the liquid in the head. Thus the joints are a sphere (of activity) allied to the tin processes. It is the articular cartilage, covering the head of the bone, within which the true bone tissue resides.

W. PELIKAN (21)

It is the synovial liquid constantly renewed by the articular capsule that stimulates the production of cartilage at the extremity of bones.

We know that in the embryo the entire bone is a cartilage formation. As growth continues the cartilage is overcome and replaced by bone formation that, proceeding from centre towards periphery, leaves only the cartilage at the joints as a last remnant. Bone and cartilage are polar opposites because of their formative impulses. The structured, almost mineral bone matter stands in contrast to the watery, homogenous, non-structured substance of the cartilage.

W. PELIKAN (22)

The liver is, in a strange manner, an organic counterpart of the tin process. The liver is primarily a plastic organ. It is really the largest gland in the body's fluid organization. From the digestive process it receives the liquefied food, while on the other hand special processes occur in the liver of densification and substance formation, such as the production of solid liver starch (glycogen) from the dissolved carbohydrates [or new proteins from the dissolved amino acids].

W. PELIKAN (23)

Tin [process] may be broadly described as a remedy that regulates opposing fields of force; on the one hand, those that appear in construction, growth and swelling (water abundance) and, on the other hand, those of solidification and drying up (tin process).

W. PELIKAN (24)

The dehydration or drying action of tin, so important in the condensation of organic substances, needs to be balanced with a good amount of water.

E. Jupiter seal

If the Saturn seal has an irradiating centre, in Jupiter we have the periphery extending inwardly interacting with a centre extending outwardly with three distinct spaces.

The external line of the Saturn seal is amplified here. The concave part has a cup-like gesture. It contains something that wants to enter. The central line responds by seven elongations that push the middle line into the convexity of the external lines. The middle line undulates around these concavities and convexities.

We have an image of a sensorial input that the centre preserves by using nerve elongations. This is the second stage of life—the life of nerves. As an etheric script, this drawing depicts membrane sensitivity—reactivity (motricity).

The outward and inward prolongations are like nerves. The peripheric line (sense impressions) penetrates the inside with sense apparatuses. From the centre a motor response is then possible. The Jupiter metabolic process has a strong influence on the nerve system. Its organ, the liver, receives from the periphery (digestion) the dismantled (soluble) substances of Nature and responds by re-constructing new substances for the spirit in incarnation.

F. Summary of the liver landscape [25]

Inner organic world
- Treasure organ: liver (anabolism)
- Workshop organ: gall bladder (catabolism)
- Associated tissue: connective tissue
- Energy tendency: start of expansion of structures—germination
- Vitality of the inner territory with envelopes surrounding the organs as well as the external movement (fascias of connective tissue)
- Dynamic of immunity (inner clean-up and defence against invaders)

At the skin level the inner world perceives, or insures the health of:
- Flavour and texture: the acidity of fermentation (sauerkraut, yoghurt). The consistence of food
- Body fluid: tears
- Transformed skin: nails

In the psychic world
- Psychic instrument: HUN, a self assertive power of survival
- Primal emotion: anger
- Negative feeling: irritability, resentment, boredom
- Vocal expression: shouting
- The health of a perceptual organ: the eyes

G. For the health of this landscape

It's important to avoid too much irritability, volcanic anger, a controlling attitude towards others or self blame—it depresses this landscape. The right side of the intestine, close to the liver, will not operate properly, and the production/evacuation of bile will be impaired. The contraction of the gall bladder without food can cause bile to attack the lining of the duodenum.

- Learn to compromise.
- Water is the primary food for the liver.
- Watch fat and protein intake—they should be digested and absorbed only in the small intestine (not in the large intestine where they produce noxious gases).
- Finish what you have started—don't be too sanguine.
- Assert a psychic and physical space for your project.
- Avoid resentment and boredom.
- Be aware that constant strong outdoor wind makes us irritable.
- Stop eating before the satiety level. Over-eating is a burden for this organ.
- Reduce toxins—they tend to accumulate in this detox organ.
- The liver opens the blood to new substances. It has an expansive effect. A little bit of acid food has a beneficial contracting effect on it.
- Stretching, especially when we get older, is important. Inner sensoriality is in the connective tissue. When we stretch the blood flow increases its nutritive presence in the hard tissues such as ligaments and tendons.
- Don't be too afraid of micro-organisms. Cats and dogs keep us

in touch with the bacteria of the environment and exercise our immune system. Through lacto-fermented food (live yoghurt, sauerkraut etc...) we repopulate the inner fauna/flora of the large intestine. In a young child the immune system will develop more strongly if the child is close to the natural world. Growing up on a farm helps to create a robust immune system.

References

1 – Rudolf Steiner in *The Fourth Dimension*, Dornach, 30 March, 1920.

2 – Idem p. 127 in Anthroposophic Press 2001.

3 – Rudolf Steiner in *Forming of Man Through Cosmic Influences* Dornach 28 Oct. – 5 Nov., 1921.

4 – On YouTube Pierre-Marie Lleba talked about neuro-genesis. He sees the hippocampus as a *'fontaine de jouvence'* of the brain stem cells that needs to be activated.

5 – Rudolf Steiner, *The Spiritual Guidance of Mankind*—three lectures by Steiner, Copenhagen, June 1911, edited by H. Collison, Rudolf Steiner Publishing Co.

6 – Rudolf Steiner in *Mystery of the Universe*, Lecture 5, 17 April, 1920.

7 – Rudolf Steiner in *The Mystery of the Universe*, Lecture 7, 9 – 16 April, 1921, Dornach.

8 – Rudolf Steiner in *Occult Science*, Chapter 2.

9 to 12 – J. L. Oschman in *Energy Medicine—The Scientific Basis.*

13 – Popp, Fritz, 2003 *Properties of Bio Photons and their Theoretical Implication*, Indian Journal of Experimental Biology, pp. 391- 402.

14 – Lynne McTaggart, *The Field.*

15 – Walter Holtzappel in *The Human Organs.*

16 – Scharrer in *Biochemistry of the Trace Elements.*

17 – R. Hauschka in *The Nature of Substance.*

18 – W. Pelican in *The Secrets of Metals.*

19 – R. Hauschka in *The Nature of Substance.*

20 – Idem.

21 – W. Pelikan in *The Secrets of Metals.*

22 – Idem.

23 – Idem.

24 – Idem.

25 – Jean-Marc Eyssalet in *Les Cinq Chemins du Clair et de L'Obscur.* Trédaniel.

CHAPTER 3
MARS PROCESS

The essence of pulsations
The beginning of the psychic world

Preamble:
A tri-unity in space emerging in time

There is a threefoldness in the progressive appearance of living creatures. This unfolds in space through a time process that we examined earlier (daily and seasonal). It always starts as a concentration of genetic material in one cell, a kind of tool box that an entelechy uses to build its own organic substances—the actualization of a potential.

In the plant kingdom the seed or bud is a **point** of potential in space. This is one meaning of the Chinese ideogram WATER: a return to the origin, a contraction to the essence.

When the conditions are favourable new **lines**—roots (geotropism) and stems (heliotropism) develop. This is one meaning of the ideogram WOOD: opening/germination. This gives rise to the rhythmic unfolding of various **surfaces**—leaves.

A leaf/surface with a bud/**point** that becomes another leaf/surface with a bud/point and so on, climbing towards the light in an anti-clockwise motion with the leaves getting smaller towards the top. This is one meaning for the FIRE ideogram: expansion in space.

A flower bud (as a metamorphic collective of surfaces) appears after the unfolding of the leaves. The leaves become a **volume** (flower) bringing a multitude of shape, colours and scents. This is one meaning of the ideogram EARTH: after receiving from the air and soil the plant starts to give aroma, pollen, nectar. In this phase of development there is an exchange (take/give) with the world.

Then a multitude of points/seeds form through genetic reproduction and dry out for future expression. This is one meaning for the METAL ideogram: drainage or the beginning of a contraction stage for preservation.

At the tip of the root/line is a living bud/**point** that explores (WOOD) the ground fertility while the roots expand (FIRE) in the fertile soil giving stability to the upright extension. Occasionally we see a cloning reproduction (EARTH) through various **volume**/tubers/bulbs. From point to volume we have the basis of geometry on the move. They are a lot of variations on this cycle.

For animals and humans it is the same. We start as a **point**/zygote that unfolds as a curved **line**/embryo containing the primitive/**surface** layers (ecto meso. and endoderm). Progressively these membrane surfaces will create a protective space for a **volume**/organ. These volume/organs are surrounded by highly sensitive **surfaces**/envelopes (pericardium for the heart, for instance). Because each organ has a specific role in regard to the whole it has to be individualized by a living membrane (often double like the serous membrane, serving the heart, lungs, etc). It is a rule in biology that an animal, plant or organ needs a semi-permeable skin or membrane to manifest its metabolic activity. To fully understand an organ we need to properly grasp its rhythmic activity as well as its neural connections and metabolic functions in relation to the whole. It is especially important to understand the way the organ changes the pulsing liquid tissues that go through it: the blood and lymph.

Mars process: The essence of pulsations and the beginning of our psychic world

A. Life of breath—formative life
B. Gall bladder and bile
C. Psychic influence: Hun
D. Metal: iron
E. Mars seal

F. Summary of the gall bladder landscape

G. For the health of this landscape

A. Life of breath—formative life

Widening the concept of breathing

> I have also pointed out what rests on these planetary alignments.
> The nerve-life comes into contact with the breathing so that
> the next stage of life, [after the life of senses and nerves], going
> inwards, is the life of breath.
>
> RUDOLF STEINER (1)

Breathing is usually associated with the lungs. When we inhale
air we contract our respiratory muscles, lower the pressure inside
and air is sucked in. The air goes out passively when the contraction stops. Physiologists call this **ventilation.** Day and night air we
breathe in moves over a lung surface of around 70 square metres.
We do this without thinking about it. This pulsed ventilation puts
us directly in touch with a huge variety of climatic influences
and aromas. Breathing air is more than just an exchange of gases.
When, for instance, we breathe the air after the rain has washed it
clear of dust, we can sense a *je ne sais quoi* that feels quite vitalizing.
Part of this freshness is due to smaller negative ions in the air after
the rain. Thanks to ventilation, we are, every second, enmeshed in
an ocean of aromas as well as the wider climatic rhythms of our
environment.

> Man's breathing is constantly renewed by something that he
> picks up in the external world, and this something benefits all
> sensorial zones.
>
> RUDOLF STEINER (2)

Every living thing has a self-maintaining interior with a primal
ability to receive impressions from the immediate environment

and to respond. Plants are sensitive to light, temperature, gravity, etc. They build a carbohydrate architecture. Animals progressively develop their sensory organs within which sentience (a capacity to think, feel and will) and increasingly conscious responses appear. Sensing with apparatuses that perceive an aspect of the external world was essential for their survival, mobility and the expression of their instinctual behaviour. With animals we see the incorporation of a proteic system of organs.

Not only the Earth, has living properties with multitude of fulcrum points amiable to life. We are also nested inside a solar system where the planets reverberate in us as organ systems.

Animals, like plants, have an **etheric** or life body that constantly rebuilds their soma (physical body). By integrating the activity of the planets inside us, Humans become a system of organs that brings capacities for a psychic world to emerge with its soul faculties. This part of our metaphysical anatomy is called an **astral body**: it is the moving planetary bodies that resonate in us. Our organs register planetary activities.

The entry of **pulsed perceptions** through ventilation and sense perception according to day/night, waking/sleeping, eating/fasting and the seasonal rhythms is part of this rhythmic connection between outside and inside.

On the other hand **respiration**, in biochemistry, is the process in which we burn sugar in the mitochondria of each cell with the help of oxygen. This release of energy in the sugar allows the creation of a protein architecture in animals. Respiration then becomes the counterpart in the animal of the photosynthetic process in plants where complex sugar (carbohydrate) architectures first emerged. Haemoglobin, as a red pigment with its iron nucleus in red blood cells, is similar to the green chlorophyll pigment—the difference is that in plants, rather than iron, magnesium is used in the nucleus in the chloroplasts green leaves. The molecular structure of both pigments is similar but the central element is different. Respiration pulses according to our need for growth or movement and is in tune with the environment.

Sensors in the aorta evaluate the acidity and oxygen pressure in the blood and convey that information to specific grey centres under the rule of our primitive reptilian brain. From there our respiratory muscles contract.

We make a distinction here between rhythmic pulsed perceptions, ventilation (air movement) and respiration (freeing of energy), each of them with their own unique rhythm. Now we need to add another essential rhythm in direct connection with the brain activity. An aspect of the Mars Process is the activation of neurons in the brain in order for our consciousness to register images. This is done through the various vital **breath-pulses** inside the brain. The influence of Mars comes as **vital beats** and **membrane tension** around the brain's grey matter. Without these beats and tensions there would be no appearance of images in our consciousness.

> In taking in the air, the breath sets [the human being] first into a kind of rhythm and this continues through the spinal column up to the brain.
>
> RUDOLF STEINER (3)

Osteopaths work with the rhythmic flow of inner liquids with a special interest in the movement of the cerebral spinal fluid (CSF) that surrounds the grey matter of the spinal chord and brain.

> From the life of breath is born not only what inhabits the consciousness but also the images of all the internal organs. The internal organs are then, through the respiratory process, formed first as images; they are not yet substantial realities …we breathe in constantly the images of our internal organization.
>
> RUDOLF STEINER (4)

The next chapter, the Sun Process, will explore the impact of sense impressions that travel inside and feed our self-maintaining interior realm. Subliminal or conscious impressions form the basis of our psyche and body landscapes. The content of sense impressions are the blueprints that form our psychic and physical life.

The Mars Process, thus, helps to reveal the contents of our impressions to our consciousness, be it a sight, sound or taste. The memories that are formed (e.g. of an event) will remain, nourishing/inhabiting our psychic world. Only one thing is needed for consciousness to grasp what is perceived by our sensorial organs (Saturn impulse) and preserved in the neurons (Jupiter impulse): a nourishing pulse (breath) imposing a rhythmic tension on membranes around the grey matter of our brain. 'Breath' refers to a sea of influences continually flowing into us.

Our vertebral column has concavity and convexity. Inside it the neural chord enveloped by the inelastic membranes (meninges) is free floating. With each breath (ventilation), we impose a change or movement in the curve of the vertebral column and it reverberates on the movement of the cerebrospinal fluid (CSF) around the spinal chord and the brain. Pulses are not material, nor are they energy. Nevertheless they are an integral part of our make-up and each organ of our body develops its own rhythmic pulsation.

> It is owing to the contact of the breathing-rhythm with the nerve-currents that we can form pictures of the outer world [in our consciousness]. Abstract thoughts depend still on the nerve-life, but the **pictorial and formative** is connected with the breathing. We can say: here we have the formative life, and since we breathe we have it in us. It lives naturally in the human form and partakes in it.
>
> RUDOLF STEINER (5)

Pictorial means that what we take in (sense impressions) serves to form our psyche; formative means that what we absorb serves to form the soma.

Let's look at **pictorial** first. When the sense perceptions become image-representations in our consciousness, we observe the formative impact they have on our psychic world. A breath-pulse needs to meet a nerve current in order for the preserved image residing in the nerve to be revealed to our consciousness. These breath-pulses are numerous.

The obvious *first pulse* comes from the blood stream. A *second* pulse is the constant creation and re-absorption of cerebrospinal fluid (CSF). The brain and spinal chord are surrounded by three layers (meninges). It is between the pia mater and the arachnoid layers that the CSF circulates. Only one cell layer of the pia mater covers the grey matter. The CSF assures an immunological protection, nurses the grey matter and puts the whole brain mass in a state of neutral buoyancy where it weighs something like 25 grams instead of its actual 1400 grams (on a scale). If the brain weren't bathed in water it would collapse on itself like a whale on a beach with no possibility for blood circulation. In Figure 1 we have a tri-dimensional illustration of the vesicles occupying the centre of the brain and producing the CSF.

Figure 1: Vesicles of cerebrospinal fluid at the centre of the brain.

Production of CSF: 500 ml. per day. Capacity: 135 to 150 ml. Turnover: replaced 3.7 times per day. Pressure: 8 to 15 mm. Hg. This pressure is constantly renewed by the plexus choroids and re-absorbed in the blood stream through the arachnoid villi.

If we reduce the pressure of this liquid too much with a lumbar puncture we lose consciousness. Swedish scientist, Emanuel Swedenborg (1688 – 1772), in c.1741 called the CSF a 'spirituous lymph'. The clear liquid of the CSF is not just protective but nourishes the grey matter and detoxes it.

Because the inelastic meningeal ligament is free floating in the vertebral column, attached at the top to the first two cervical vertebrae and at the bottom to the sacrum, the CSF inside will go in a state of suction/pressure each time we ventilate allowing its movement up and down as a *third* pulse. Our daily movements will also stretch this ligament, varying the tension.

Pressure on bone crystalline structure (carrying heavy loads) produces piezoelectricity that stimulates the osteocytes to produce denser bones. So is stretching of the connective tissue membranes. For an exact note to come from a violin string the tension needs to be right. Our internal membrane made of connective tissues are all the time under various tension. Having already a semi-conductive property, stretching the meninges creates an essential membrane tension vital for the nourishment of the grey matter *(fourth pulse)*.

Note 1—Neuroglial cells

The health of the brain depends directly on neuroglial cells. Unlike neurons, neuroglial cells can reproduce. There's a principle in physiology: *if you don't use an organ, it atrophies.* So if the brain doesn't receive or give enough sensory-motor impulses, the neuroglial cells will stop growing and reproducing thus damaging the scaffolding of the brain.

The neuroglial cells of the nervous system are a kind of specialized connective tissue. They reproduce easily if they are stimulated. And the stimulation comes from the sensorial and motor activity of the neurons. There are many different types of neuroglial cells, here are a few of them:

A – The **astrocytes** play an active role in feeding the neurons as well as participating in the blood/brain barrier. They make connections between neurons and capillaries forming the basic scaffolding of the grey matter. Their ways to surround the capillaries in the brain are very similar to the podocytes in the nephron of the kidneys. The virtual liquid they provide to the neurons moves because of their pulsing activity.

B – The **microglial cells** are little macrophages digesting dead brain cells. Where a neuron is connected with hundreds of others when it dies, then these cells play a role in reconnecting the living neurons together.

C – Every neuronal extension (axon) is surrounded by a mantle (myelin sheath of phospholipids) produced by the **oligodendrocytes** in the brain and the **Schwann cells** in the peripheric nervous system.

D – **Pituicytes** that store oxytocin and vasopressin (made in the hypothalamus) in the posterior pituitary. They are similar to astrocytes with their many extensions.

E – **Ependimal cells** producing the cerebrospinal fluid (CSF) in the plexus choroids of the ventricles.

F – **Satellites cells** more active in the little brains (ganglia) of the autonomic nervous system (ANS) present in the thorax and abdomen.

In each kidney, we have one million nephrons or renal corpuscles filtering the blood stream. The **podocytes**, like the astrocytes in the brain, surround the capillaries and act as a kidney/blood barrier allowing an aspect of the blood to become a filtrate (the first step in the formation of urine). Here the amoeba-like cells act as separators allowing blood purification.

A fifth pulse can be found in the astrocytes of the neuroglial cells (Note 1) of the brain. The astrocytes, one of the glia cells, link the blood vessels to the neurons and constantly pulse to activate the virtual liquid of this organ. They also hold the 'scaffolding' of the brain, keeping the millions of nerves from touching one another. We have ten times more neuroglial cells than neurons, responsible for the health of the 'aquarium' in which the neurons bathe. Astrocytes, that are part of the blood-brain barrier, nurse the neurons by extracting nourishment from the capillaries. They can reproduce as long as the brain is kept alive through sensory and motor activity.

> In a normal state of consciousness we never think and form concepts of our environment merely by a process connected with the nerves and senses, but a stream of breath [pulsation] is always flowing through this process. We think inasmuch as our breath is continually surging and streaming through our nerves and senses.
>
> RUDOLF STEINER (6)

> And it is due to the breath [pulses] that not only man's conscious breathing is the outcome, but that pictures of all the inner organs [bringing the seven metabolic processes from the planets] arise in imitation of the outer form. Thus, in the first place, the inner organs are formed as pictures by way of the breathing processes.
>
> RUDOLF STEINER (7)

> 'They are not yet substantial'—the breath pulse reveals first a picture of the inner man before the soma is formed. 'As we move with the Earth in the zodiac [and planets] we are all the time inhaling the pictures [through sense perception] of our inner organization. We breathe them [impressions] in from the external world [even subliminally].'
>
> RUDOLF STEINER (8)

The word picture meaning 'not yet substantial' can be seen here as a blueprint of creation like an architectural plan for a building. If we breathe in these pictures constantly through our sense perceptions, it means that we can be recreated all the time. The physiological fact is that our physical organs are themselves constantly being rebuilt.

The Sun is instrumental in bringing these formative pictures by directing these subtle influences from the stars and planets towards Earth. Rudolf Steiner pointed out several times that we should think of the Sun as a hole in the fabric of space/time connecting it with counter space. It attracts these spiritual formative forces from the Solar System and channels them towards Earth in a rhythmic way. (See Sun Process—Reference 1.) Light from the Sun is not just electromagnetic frequencies but also carries the subtle blueprint of Creation.

An inside consciousness in progress

As shown in the study of embryology, all Vertebrates have a similar start. For instance, the ends of the limbs always have five digits. These embryonic elongations develop in various ways (fins, wings, paws, hands) according to the animal group. In horses, the specialization reaches a point where the animal walks on their toe nail (hence the term ungulates). In Primates and humans the development of our hands remains at an unspecialized stage of development, making us much more versatile.

Does consciousness undergo a similar unfolding in the history of Humankind or even in the development of an individual human being? Is consciousness present before the moment of conception? Do we make proper distinctions between intelligent activities and consciousness in this era of increasingly sophisticated artificial intelligence?

One thing is certain, it is because of these various pulses around our grey matter that consciousness emerges inside us and uses various faculties to operate in this dense world. One such faculty transforms sense impressions into concepts/words (rational thinking intelligence). Then we can also translate the outer world into colours, music... expressions (artistic feeling intelligence). The most primeval faculty allows us to survive by transforming the outer world to fulfil our need for shelter, food, clothes... (craftsman willing intelligence).

Step by step consciousness evolves from baby to adult. At the beginning the newborn doesn't feel any separation from the world. The conscious mental activity will develop progressively. He is initially 'at one' with the surrounding in a pre-mental state. There is an archaic-magical side to this where everything perceived is received with wonder. And because the 'I Am' inside wants to relate with what he perceives, the baby starts to master his musculoskeletal system to move and grasp the World. Even if a child might feel the beginning of an 'I' and 'Thou' in early childhood, the consciousness is still attached to a family or tribe with its uses and customs, language... The baby grows fast and its will/metabolic energy is totally consecrated to this task. Its psychic tendency is to live more in the realm of images than abstract concepts.

In adolescence, with the start of sexual activity, we sense that the psyche makes an effort to harmonize with the wider world. The mind is in search of coherence, and self-consciousness is developing. This separation is not achieved without rebellion.

Then, with the rational/abstract mind-consciousness developing, the ego is alone in the world. This intellect soul consciousness has developed in the last few centuries leaving behind the old religious myths and leading towards the techno civilization we have now where we try to explain everything with the concept of matter and energy (materialism).

The next step can be taken in a human life if a human being perceives that in fact no separation between the outer and inner world exists. This is the search for a more integral consciousness beyond the strict intellectual one. Then a participatory (stewardship) consciousness can integrate its activity with the Natural World, and a co-evolution is possible.

German philosopher, Jean Gebser (1905 – 1973) in *The Ever Present Origin* and British philosopher, Owen Barfield (1898 – 1997) in *History in English Words,* both studied the evolution of human consciousness through history. It seems that the development of the human psyche resumes this path of human consciousness through various civilizations in history.

The entry of perceived images leads towards the formation of words-sounds. Barfield argued that:

The standard understanding of the evolution of language is that all words referring to something spiritual or abstract have their origin in literal meaning (original perception)...Throughout the recorded history of language the movement of meaning has been from concrete to abstract.

Concrete here means that the original sounds reflected intelligent activities of the Beings of things observed and ancient people preferred to use pictograms like Chinese ideograms that are closer to their subtle perceptions. For them these activities were intelligent entities (Beings or Deities). They were akin to vectors of activity in geometry.

On the other hand, abstract means that, over time, words-sounds lost their original roots and became 'petrified metaphors' written with letters.

In *The Harmony of the Human Body* Armin Husemann states:

> The world of Ideas from which we take the concept we combine with sensorial perception is, as we noted in the introductory chapters, the etheric world. Which is why Rudolf Steiner describes the etheric world as flooded with cosmic thoughts.

From perception to memory

We saw that sensorial organs (Saturn) are linked with nerve prolongations (Jupiter) that preserve the sensation on the surface of the brain where various beats and membrane tension (Mars) are essential for the sensation to become a conscious image. We observe that the perception is stored as a memory-picture that can be retrieved.

Neuro-physiologists still hope to find the memory storage area in the brain. People have often noted that when we move we can learn by heart more quickly, or, if you give a lecture, the memory of what you have to say flows better if you move. Is it possible that not just the brain but the whole etheric body is used to store this information? One thing seems clear: the images of things and their memories in our consciousness are not energy or matter.

On the one hand, images are the reflections in us of the Beings of things; they are thought forms that the brain, as a transducer, captures. This activity creates our unique psychic world. On the other hand, the body is constantly rebuilt in its somatic aspect with the presence of the builders of all trades (elementals). (See Mercury Process—Lung ideogram.) This process is deep in our unconscious; this is the realm of the will. It is this etheric vehicle that integrates the fine aspects of food and air (see Saturn Process—Spleen). Is there a link between these two subtle bodies (astral body—psyche / etheric body—soma) that enables memory to remain in us?

> Now, if we have something which impresses upon the ether-body our memory-pictures taken, as it were, from the soul, and if from the other side we recognize the ether-body as that supersensible expression of our organism which is nearest to the physical and built it, the question then arises: How does this impressing come about? In other words, when the human being works over external impressions, makes them into memory-pictures, and in doing so thrusts them into his ether-body, how does it happen that he does actually bring down into the ether-body what the astral body has first worked over and what now presses against the ether-body? How does he transfer it?
>
> RUDOLF STEINER (9)

Two streams—**one,** from up downwards, comes from the integration of outside forces present in us as images that develop our psychic world; **the other one,** from down upwards, comes from the integration of imponderables in air and food. Just as we transform food in order to build our own unique soma, we also need to integrate the subtle resonances of what comes in through the lungs and digestive organs. (See Venus Process.) These two streams meet in the brain at specific loci. Memories of the first few years of life are very patchy because these two streams don't yet meet with full intensity. (Figure 2—Two Streams.)

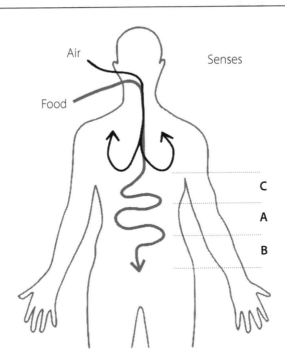

Figure 2: Two Streams

The meeting of two streams

1 – Whatever enters us through conscious sensorial impressions forms the basis of our psychic world. From the pre-mental state of the newborn baby the sensorial perceptions will elaborate his inner psyche: no sensation means no psychic development. In order to unfold various ways to transform the world (soul faculties of thinking, feeling and willing), the mind needs to be fed by inner and outer perceptions. The stream that creates the psyche condenses its activity in the pineal gland that tends to form a kind of crystalline sand over time.

2 – Another more unconscious stream of impressions from our rhythmic relation with air and food emerges not so much as pictorial but formative for the soma. This stream of influences has to be digested like material food. This integration

of the subtle aspect of air (YANG CHI) and food (GU CHI) is performed by the etheric morphic field of the organs of the thorax and abdomen. It is important that the energetic resonance of substances, such as an aroma, is mingled with our unique ancestral energy (YUAN CHI) before flowing through the body. When this integration is done the new current (ZHEN CHI) flows in liquids and meridians. It also condenses around the hypothalamus/hypophysis gland, a few centimetres from the pineal gland.

A – The spleen sphere acts as a captor of influences especially from air and food. (*Explained in Saturn Process—spleen.*)

B – The kidney sphere integrates these influences with our own make-up. (*Explained in Venus Process—kidney.*)

C – The heart sphere distributes the newly formed energetic current (liquid light). (*Explained in Sun Process—heart.*)

The system responsible for this digestive/distribution activity is part of the complex organization of the etheric body and is called The Triple Warmer (integrator) coupled with The Master of the Heart (distributor) in Chinese physiology.

This transfer takes place in a very remarkable way. If we observe the blood—let us now imagine ourselves within the human ether-body—quite schematically as it courses through the heart, and think of it as the external physical expression of the human ego, we thereby see how this ego works, how it receives impressions corresponding with the outer world and condenses these to memory-pictures. We see, furthermore, not only that our blood is active in this process, but also that, throughout its course, especially in the upward direction, somewhat less in the downward, it stirs up the ether-body, so that **we see currents developing everywhere in the ether-body** [meridians], taking a very definite course, as if they would join the blood flowing upward from the heart and go up to the head.

RUDOLF STEINER (10)

(See Sun Process—heart area / Venus Process—kidney area.)

Chinese physiology is clear about this last subtle current going upward. Not only the sense organs capture images but the spleen, this cup of flesh, gathers, like an aerial, the subtle emissions of the world outside especially from air and food. These need to be integrated into our own make-up. The subtle energetic aspect of air and food (CHI) first go from the spleen to the kidneys area to be integrated with our own ancestral energy (see the Venus Process—kidney area). Then it surges like an etheric fountain towards the heart circulation (see the Sun Process—heart area) where this renewed energy starts to move into the meridians, the lymphatic system, the blood and the cerebrospinal fluid (CSF). This dual etheric system is called the Triple Warmer (a digester integrator) and the Master of the Heart (an energizing distributor) in Chinese physiology.

So we have one current from the etheric body and another current from the images perceived consciously by the astral body.

> And in the head these currents come together, in about the same way, to use a comparison belonging to the external world, as do currents of electricity when they rush towards a point which is opposed by another point, so as to neutralize the positive and the negative. When we observe with a soul trained in occult methods, we see at this point ether-forces compressed as if under a very powerful tension, those ether-forces which are called forth through the impressions that now desire to become definite concepts, memory-pictures, and to stamp themselves upon the ether-body.
>
> RUDOLF STEINER (11)

(See Figure 1—Two Streams.)

> Thus we have in the brain, whenever a memory-picture forms itself, two ether currents, one coming from below [the breathing/ digesting CHI integrated with our ancestral energy] and one from above [integrated sense perceptions that will be conscious

pictures in the soul]. These oppose each other under the greatest possible tension, just as two electric currents oppose each other. If a balance is brought about between these two currents, then a concept has become a memory-picture and has incorporated itself in the ether body.

RUDOLF STEINER (12)

Such supersensible currents in the human organism always express themselves by creating for themselves also a physical sense-organ, which we must first look upon as a sense-manifestation. Thus we have within us an organ, situated in the centre of the brain, which is the physical sense-expression for that which will take the form of a memory-picture.

RUDOLF STEINER (13)

For a sense impression to become a memory, consciousness must be there and this organ is one point of integration.

'...and opposite to this is situated still another organ in the brain'. This other organ gathers all that has been integrated by the subtle sensoriality of air and food. (See Venus Process.)

These two organs in the human brain are the physical-sensible expression of the two currents in the human ether-body; they are, one might say, something like the ultimate indication of the fact that there are such currents in the ether-body. **These currents condense themselves with such force that they seize the human bodily substance and consolidate it into these (two) organs. We thus actually get an impression of bright etheric light-currents** [liquid light] streaming across from the one to the other of these organs, and pouring themselves out over the human ether-body (*meridians*). These organs are actually present in the human organism. One of them is the *pineal gland;* the other, the so-called *pituitary body* [the master hormonal gland]. [The 'epiphysis' and 'hypothalamus-hypophysis' respectively.] We have here, at a definite point in the human physical organism, the external physical expression of the co-operation of soul [astral] and [etheric] body!

RUDOLF STEINER (13)

From the first current emerges our unique *psyche* with its memory and the second current (etheric) builds our unique *soma*. They spark in us every second of our life.

With these continuous sparks, memory is stored in our etheric organization all over the body. It is well known that we memorize faster when on the move. When we need to give a talk we also gather thought forms, memories, ideas much faster when we walk. Movement activates the interface between the physical and the etheric vehicle that rebuilds it constantly. By doing so, movement gives a better access to stored memory-pictures.

> What exactly is the surface of the organs? It is nothing less than a reflecting apparatus for our soul life. What we perceive and also what we digest with our thinking is reflected upon the surface of all our organs; this reflection represents our memories, during life. Thus, our memory is what is reflected upon the outer surface of the heart, lungs and spleen, and our other organs after we have perceived and digested it in our thinking. The surface of the lungs [and pleura] is especially sensitive to abstract idea...
>
> ...in thoughts through which we form images of outer objects, these forces are, in a certain way, stored in the lungs.

RUDOLF STEINER (14)

The play of fancy

The Beings of things resonate in us through our sense perceptions and we can memorize the experience. This forms the beginning of our psychic life where various pictures of the world lodge. As a psychic tool from the spleen landscape, (see Saturn Process) the YI or mind is not only a gatherer of thoughts, insights and memories, but is always in search of a coherent set of ideas that interpret the world perceived. After all, we live in a universe that has coherence.

The history of Humankind is full of ideologies that stimulated the creation of civilization and empires bringing great progress in art and science. But ideologies, we observe, can justify all kinds of atrocities. English poet William Blake (1757 – 1827) was aware that they can become 'mind-forged manacles', full of rigid dogma. Many aspects of human history are very brutal, revealing human beings to be not as evolved or civilized as we might hope but only 'half-decent' creatures.

Human beings still have a lot of animality to master and shadowy elemental forces to cope with (see the Mercury Process—Lung area). The forces of intentional destruction exist only in the soul of Humans, not in Nature. It is not about denying or repressing this animality but acknowledging the power it gives us. In the liver-gall bladder landscape there is a strong self-assertive power. For the sake of survival the tendency is there to accumulate for the benefit of the family, group or clan. This trait has a positive aspect. Its negative aspect is greed that grabs more for its own sake or to control others.

Besides ideologies common to all human groups, human beings have the pack-animal pecking order tendency ingrained deep in our psyche. There have always been individuals or groups leading communities and forming hierarchies. There's nothing wrong with having power. But the use of power without empathy is tyranny. Power can seduce its wielder and encourage a negative aspect—greed.

Looking at various civilizations through history, the tendency to accumulate more power has always been there in the human soul. We are living on Earth in a cosmos of wisdom. Humanity's task is to develop brotherhood and this has to be achieved by every person on Earth. The third common denominator of all groups working together is the accumulation of a plus-value: meaning that groups of people over time produce more then they need. It can be clothes, food or money. Historically, this plus value is normally kept by a ruling class for their sole benefit.

The Indian sage Gautama Buddha (circa sixth to fifth century BCE) named the three main calamities of the human soul:

ignorance, greed and cruelty. The central Christian command-
ment—to love one another—is at the basis of Christianity. The
day it is applied—taking care of one another—we will be close to
universal brotherhood. Only the Higher Self or Spirit expressed
through the soul faculties can tame our innate animality. Aristotle
called this spirit Entelechia, and in Chinese physiology it is the
complex image of SHEN (the creative spirit).

The future will see our current civilization as the most barbaric
one with its dire weapons (cluster bombs, nuclear weapons,
chemical weapons) and technology that doesn't favour bio-
diversity of life. Facing the sickness of Nature and human societies, there is only one thing that is left to do as transient citizens of
the Earth: healing.

B. Gall bladder and bile

The ideogram for gall bladder is DAN and has to do with deci-
siveness that is part of the psychic entity of the liver landscape:
the HUN or self-assertive drive of every living creature. The gall
bladder is the liver's workshop organ (see Intro about workshop
and treasure organs).

The gall bladder is intimately connected with the largest gland of the
body: the liver. More than a bag nesting under and inside the liver,
its ducts enter the microscopic structure of a multitude of liver lobules organized in hexagonal frames resembling a beehive. From tiny
canals the bile produced by the hepatocytes (liver cells) is drained
out of the liver towards the sphincter of Oddi in the duodenum.
When this sphincter is closed, due to the absence of food coming out
of the stomach, the bile refluxes to the gall bladder where it will be
concentrated (10x) into a highly potent alkaline green-yellow viscous
liquid in order to emulsify fat. The liquid re-absorbed by this workshop organ will go back to the liver and be reused in a constant daily
excretory process. Production of bile: around one litre a day by the
liver and concentrated by up to ten times by the gall bladder. This
organ also touches the main breathing muscle: the diaphragm.

With bile we have a powerful warrior tool to emulsify (fragment) fat which has a tendency to coat or enclose other substances. For example, if we plunge our hand in warm oily water, very quickly the fat will envelop our hand. Water is insufficient to remove this fatty coating; we need soap which is itself made of oil transformed by a strong alkaline substance to wash it off.

Proteins and carbohydrates, both covered with oil in our food, render enzymatic activities nearly impossible. Bile frees these proteins and carbohydrates and allows them to be digested in the small intestine. Without bile they would have to be digested in the large intestine by bacteria. We can't digest complex sugars like cellulose but the bacteria in the gut can. By-products of this bacterial digestion are various gases like CO_2. The less bile we produce the more of these proteins and fats will have be digested in the gut producing noxious gases (sulphuric 'indol' type), poisonous for our system.

Fat has another interesting property: it absorbs and holds the subtle fragrance of things. Perfumers use fats and oils to extract the odour and vital essence of things. Put uncovered butter in a fridge next to the rest of your fish casserole, and it won't be long before you have fishy butter. The fat we eat carries a huge array of **flavours that ought not to be underestimated in their formative properties** *(JING CHI such as flavours as energy)*. We will decipher JING CHI ideogram later in this chapter. The flavour of food has a huge impact on our internal organs, and the liver is the first to receive these subtle essences through the portal vein that carries the blood passing through the digestive system, the spleen and the gall bladder.

Fat (lipid) really starts to be deconstructed when the bile transforms it into a multitude of minuscule droplets of oil (emulsified) in the duodenum. With emulsification, the enveloping effect of fat descends into a microscopic level (micelles and liposomes) where enzymes can start to operate with full capacity in the small intestine to finalize our production of milky chyme for assimilation in the bloodstream.

The gall bladder, by providing concentrated bile, doesn't only emulsify the fat but creates the fluid ground with the pancreatic juice for efficient enzymatic work and absorption. The composition of bile is quite unusual. Its salts (steroid acids—tarrocolic and glycolic) can be hydrophilic (mixes with water) or lipophilic (mixed with fats), making fat and diverse oily vitamins (A, D, E, K) soluble. In an aqueous solution, depending on temperature, the bile's phospholipids (lecithin) can form monolayers (micelles), bi-layers (liposomes) or lamellar structures around nutrients. All of which have an important role in digestion and nutrient assimilation. (15)

The pigment bilirubin in the bile is a remnant of the haemoglobin pigment that has to be excreted, colouring our faeces on the yellow/brown side of the spectrum.

Cholesterol is a waxy steroid of fat made by the liver and is an important component of bile. All cells need it as a structural component of cellular membranes, allowing permeability. It is also the precursor of steroid hormones (cortisol, aldosterone and sex hormones). We eliminate cholesterol through the digestive system. Its homeostasis or stable state in our body is still not entirely understood.

With the liver and gall bladder, we can see a complex sensing system with hormonal responses in place right at the beginning of the digestive system. This hormonal system from the digestive organs regulates the secretion of various liquids that are going to digest the food to create a nourishing milk (chyme).

When we are born we need our mother's milk. Then we progressively learn to produce our own milky chyme. Litres of juices, such as bile, are needed to dismantle the organic outer world and reduce it to its simplest soluble organic forms. Amino and fatty acids, glycerine and simple sugars form the whiteness of this milk. Most of this deconstructed matter enters the blood stream and is directed towards the liver, accompanied by taste and aroma, vitamins, minerals, hormones, pigments…that impact on the function of organs. They are energetic substances.

Widening the concept of energy

The word energy means a force in action. It is the capacity for a system to modify the state of another system.

All sensory impressions are energy. They produce percept images in our consciousness (psyche) and in our blood as surely as if a tablet carries them into the organism (soma). There is a critical need to widen the concept of energy in science but this is difficult because it often goes against mainstream medicine.

It means that our health and wellbeing is directly affected by what we see and hear in a more important way than generally assumed. To hear beautiful music or live in a beautiful home surrounded by aesthetically pleasing art or architecture has an impact on our health. It is not just a case of appreciation or relaxation; perceiving these things has a direct impact on the health of our inner landscape and therefore of our whole being.

> ... a physics arose (mid nineteenth century) that sees the salvation of physics in considering physical facts separately from the human being. This is indeed the principal characteristic of modern physics. Many publications proclaim this idea as necessary for the advancement of physics, stating that nothing must be introduced that comes from the human being himself... that has to do with his own organic processes. But in this way we shall arrive at nothing.
>
> RUDOLF STEINER (16)

Traditional Chinese medicine considered sense impressions as a kind of Chi (energy force) because it impacts on the activity of organs and created ideograms as images of these activities. The ideograms stand for an inner process rather than a concept or object in space. *To grasp an ideogram we need to set in motion an image of the process in our feeling life. To 'set in motion' is the essence of CHI.*

> Life processes are in constant movement and cannot be grasped with the 'closed' mind suitable for calculation; you require

concepts mobile in themselves—pictures. The etheric man within the fluid man is apprehended in pictures.

RUDOLF STEINER (17)

Let's take the sense of smell as an example. This is the only sense that goes direct to our frontal lobe of the brain without being filtered. It is amazing that a very small patch at the roof of our nose can identify aromas by the thousands. We smell gases in the air that comes from the most evanescent part of objects. We have all experienced the onion aroma. We are not only conscious of it through our sense of smell but it also has a direct effect on our tear ducts. This aroma is a gaseous molecular architecture invading the air and impacting on our conscience and our eyes. It is the smallest signature of the onion. But the aroma of all things goes further. Being a gas they can penetrate biological membrane and invade the blood stream directly carrying their energy. Plant aromas are highly volatile and combustible because they contain hydrogen as their main element. They can't act on the form of an organ or its renewal but they impact directly on its metabolic function by increasing or decreasing its activity.

Even though we taste things in our mouth, smell is very often the main determinant of a recognized flavour. We can taste only a handful of different flavours, the main accepted ones being sweet, acid, spicy, bitter (astringent) and salty. This is the conscious part of it. For instance, a bitter substance, like sloes, will have the effect of drying out our mouth. It bites and prevents the saliva from flowing. But the thing we don't realize is this drying out effect will be carried away into all corners of our internal environment by the blood stream. Tastes stimulate organs. They contract or expand the internal activity of organs. All aspects of Chinese dietetics are based on this polarity. (18)

To heal our body where each organ has a specialized internal function of contracting or expanding the blood, we need to find in the external world a substance possessing the opposite activity that can balance the organ function. In the example above where bitterness contracts the flesh of the mouth, the main beneficiary organ will be the heart because it brings the blood into expansion. We can say that the heart in its explosive nature needs a bit of bitterness to calm it down. In the same way, because the activity of the kidney contracts the blood, it will need a substance such as salt, that lets the saliva flow in our mouth: the opposite effect to bitter. Of course too much of any basic taste can damage the internal activities of organs.

> The vegetal nature [not the digested substances but their taste/ aroma] can only act on the activities related to the functions of the organs...and can't act at all on the matter side of these organs. The activity of plants [not the substances but the process of a plant, such as its taste] is important especially when organs act in an abnormal way...when we have for instance a hyper-activity [or under-activity] in organs.
>
> RUDOLF STEINER (19)

JING and JING CHI [20]

We saw how bile releases the JING CHI of the food or its subtle aroma and oscillating qualities such as vitamins and minerals. Defining the ideogram JING is quite a task. In general terms it is a formative life principle.

Let's take human creativity as a starting point. If someone (a Spirit) makes the decision to create a specific sculpture—it is a will intention. Then more decisions need to be taken. Questions will arise as to the types of material, size, colour, position, where it's going to be shown. This is the level of images or JING. The intention and the images have a real existence in the psyche but it is **not energy or matter**. It is a **potential for action; the form doesn't yet exist in space.** A self-conscious will/intention creates the active potential—JING = the blueprint.

JING is involved in the creative process of the Universe. For the ancient Chinese JING belongs to the Anterior Heaven (spiritual). It is the realm of the Hierarchies generated by God in Christian theology, a realm of mighty Beings presiding as architects of the natural and psychic world. Other mystical traditions have their own pantheons expressing the same idea. Nevertheless this super-sensible world is not a static world forever the same. It co-evolves with the natural and psychic world (Posterior material Heaven). JING can be compared to the blueprint of the architect, alive and directional, in the psyche of the craftsmen building the house. It is the formative force of the constellations and planets raying down on Earth with the sun-rays (source of the light and warmth ether). Gold has always been considered the metal of the Sun. When sunlight goes through a thin sheet of gold we see turquoise, which is an aspect of the ideogram JING the blue green of Nature.

Steiner in *The World of the Senses and the World of the Spirit* (1911) invited us to grasp an important definition:

'...all matter is a heap of ruins of the spirit, is shattered spirit'.

'If spirit breaks into the void then mineral matter results.'

'...a breaking in pieces that does not go into the void but, for example into an etheric corporality that is already there, [like the Earth at a certain stage of its development]...plant matter originates.'

So it is for animal substances where the possibility to develop a system of proteic organs that reflects the activity of the living planet system (astral body).

'Natural objects are sculpted matter', said Ernst Marti (German doctor). (21) There is a will intention first to descend in the realm of density and follows the original architectural blueprint of creation: JING—the **Formative Forces**. They come down and create *forms* in matter (the four kingdoms)—there are manifold elemental spirits—following this blueprint of incarnation. All aspects of the four kingdoms of Nature are forms of Spirit descending in the realm of density with the help of elementals ethers. Any form can be seen as a stabilized flow of matter in resonance with its own field or pattern of tonality. This **physical matter** in form presents itself with a molecular architecture that oscillates, resonates. This oscillating activity is a **process** (JING CHI)—a vector of activation of bio-chemical function in the living. Process is then Formative Forces in matter. These **four principles** are never isolated in Nature. If form and matter are physical, formative force and process are etheric. Nevertheless human beings can isolate a mineral or plant process through dilution and succussion, allowing water to hold its oscillation for a while. Homeopathy and other potentized medicines are based on this premise.

All substances that we absorb possess internal forces, obey their own laws, have their own oscillating movements: a 'breath' as a specific irradiating molecular architecture. The ancient Chinese tradition called them (JING CHI). Our nose and tongue can capture an aspect of these 'breaths'. It can be the essential oil of rose or the bitter taste of coffee. The bile is essential to free this JING CHI from the food.

Our body continually dilutes and succusses substances (see Venus Process—Kidneys and Sun Process—Heart). With digested glucides, protides and lipids, our body transforms them into our own substances. They are our material fabrics. Many substances (minerals like manganese or even aromas, for instance) resonate in small concentrations. Biology is a science studying life. Consequently, it is relevant to acquire knowledge of the Beings of things, their formative forces or breaths and their impact on bio-chemical processes. So many diluted substances act in us through their oscillating power (breath).

> We are continually receiving impressions and the sum of all the impressions you receive is related to the portion of them which becomes a permanent conscious possession of our soul [psyche]…all the countless impressions that come into our soul from without and do not come into his consciousness, work upon the whole human being [soma]. Everything in his environment works continually upon man in his totality.
>
> RUDOLF STEINER (22)

If contemplative meditation of whatever we focus on reaches an attitude of surrender a human being 'cannot help being moved to feel a mood of balance—a balance that is not dead but quick with life; we might compare it to a gentle and even flow of water…And it is the same with every taste, smell and every sense perception; they inevitably call up in his soul a feeling of inner movement and activity. There is no colour and no tone that doesn't speak to him;…not with judgement or opinion but with living movement. In short, a time comes for such a man when the whole world of senses flings off, as it were, its disguise and reveals itself to him as something he cannot describe with any other word than will. … Everything in the world of senses is will, a strong and powerful current of will. … The world of the senses thus becomes, as it were, a sea of infinitely differentiated will.' (23) This is part of the meaning of the ideogram JING CHI.

For the one practising contemplative meditation 'having experienced all the previous stages leading to surrender—the stages we have called feeling oneself in harmony with the wisdom of the world, and before that reverence, and before that wonder—then through the penetration of these [feeling] conditions into the last gained condition of surrender, he learns how to grow together with the objects with his etheric body also, which stands behind the physical body.' (24)

The Greek Water Element (liquid state and chemical/sound ether predominates here (see Chap. 2—Jupiter Process at the end of section A—the liver).

C. Psychic influence: HUN

The gall bladder, as a representative of Mars Process, is the workshop organ of the liver and consequently has the same creative spirit and reactivity: the HUN—see previous chapter on Jupiter Process.

D. Metal related to Mars : iron [25]

Iron in nature

It permeates the earth everywhere—rocks, soil and water, and it is thought to be the most abundant metals on Earth forming as much as one third of the Earth's core. It is also one of the main elements in meteorites which continually rain down through the atmosphere.

Iron likes to combine with a huge range of elements, and wherever water, sulphur, oxygen, carbon dioxide, phosphates and silver display their actions in life processes, iron easily follows. It is very auspicious to life.

Iron has a small atomic number and is close to carbon in the Periodic Table; it is the only metal that relates with carbon. Pure molten iron dissolves carbon and creates cast iron and stainless steel.

In connection with oxygen, iron can be bivalent or trivalent, going back and forth according to circumstances. It is a breather among the metals, taking oxygen (ferric compounds) and giving off oxygen (ferrous compounds).

Iron in us

Of all the iron in the body, 66% is in the haemoglobin of the red blood cells and the rest is in the muscles, liver and spleen, and acts as a co-factor for enzyme activity. As part of the cytochromes, it participates in the ATP formation (energy made directly available). A cytochrome is a red proteic pigment containing iron, able to go from a reduced state ($Fe\ 2+$) to an oxidized state ($Fe\ 3+$). These cytochromes are involved in the respiration chain where adenosine tri-phosphate is produced (Note 2).

Note 2—Adenosine Tri-Phosphate (ATP)

Sugar is a good source of fuel, when burned it will produce, amongst other things, heat and light. In our cells the mitochondria (our little furnaces) burn sugar but the heat and light is captured by phosphoric molecules and distributed where it is needed in the cells to build proteins. Phosphorus is well known to capture, hold for a while and give away the light. In its organic form adenosine tri-phosphate (ATP) is doing the same thing.

Iron has to do with the cyclic use of energy in living creatures. If the green chlorophyll pigments in plants harvest light energy (photosynthesis) and produce sugar, the red haemoglobin pigments in animals provide oxygen to the cell for the burning of sugar that releases new energy for proteic construction. Both pigments are similar crystalline proteins, with magnesium at the centre of the green pigment and iron in the red pigment. Iron is an essential co-factor in the formation of the green pigment in the plant. It helps plants to form their light organs (green chlorophyll in their chloroplasts) that start the great adventure of the plant kingdom. Magnesium is essential for the formation of haemoglobin.

Because red blood cells live only three weeks, the spleen digests them and the pigment (bilirubin) has to be disposed of by the bile.

Iron when associated with copper is also involved in the creation of melanin that helps us digest light (suntan).

E. Mars seal

The peripheral line is minimalist in this seal. In the Saturn and Jupiter seals the periphery interplays with the middle and internal line. In the Mars seal there is a greater focus towards the centre, whereas the external line is just pulsating breath, like flying birds at the horizon. The middle lines are budding shafts that fan out at the ends, pointing towards the centre. The main gesture of the third internal line is to embrace the seed shafts in containers that touch each other.

The Mars impulse is the revealing of impressions to our conscious centre because of a breathing pulsation around the grey matter. Is it not what is happening when a sense impression (Saturn), preserved by the nerve activity (Jupiter), becomes an inner imprisoned image (Mars) in our conscious centre? We capture outside images and they become confined in our consciousness and memorized. These captured sensorial impressions are the basis of our consciousness (psyche) in an envelope of flesh. In a young baby, a pre-ego stage where everything is one, the mental starts to activate. Sensorial deprivation (used as a war tactic for torture and interrogation) leads, temporarily, towards a black-out of memory and sense of self.

In the older baby, word-sounds and concepts will emerge. Of course we can always add to the content of a concept. Our psychic life is built on this process so that our consciousness can use the psychic faculties (thinking, feeling and willing) to achieve a destiny. This reception of images in a child is the beginning of the establishment of his psychic world. The integration of images gives us a lifetime of exercise for our mind which is in constant search for coherence.

F. Summary of the gall bladder landscape

(See Chapter 2—liver landscape F.)

G. For the health of this landscape

(See Chapter 2 G.)

References

1– Rudolf Steiner, *Forming of Man through Cosmic Influences,* Lecture 2, 29 Oct, 1921, Dornach (RLXXVI vol. 1).

2 – Rudolf Steiner in *Occult Physiology.*

3 – Rudolf Steiner, Lecture 2, 29 Oct., 1921, Dornach (RLXXVI vol.) .

4 – Idem.

5 – Idem.

6 – Idem.

7 – Rudolf Steiner in *Occult Physiology, 23* March, 1911 (G 128) Chap. 4.

8 – Rudolf Steiner in *Anthroposophical Leading Thoughts.*

9 to 13 – Rudolf Steiner in *Occult Physiology.*

14 – Rudolf Steiner in *Psychoanalysis and Spiritual Psychology—Organic Processes and Soul Life,* 2 July, 1921.

15 – Gerard J. Tortora and Nicholas P. Anagnostakos in *Principles of Anatomy and Physiology,* Harper and Row.

16 – Rudolf Steiner in *The Warmth Course* , Lecture XI, Stuttgart, 9 March, 1920.

17 – Rudolf Steiner in *Occult Physiology.*

18 – See Jean-Marc Eyssalet in *Dans L'ocean des Saveurs, L'intention du Corps.*

19 – Rudolf Steiner in *Occult Physiology,* 28 March, 1911.

20 – Jean-Marc Eyssalet (see Introduction reference 9).

21 – Victor Bott, Paul Coroze and Ernst Marti in *Les Forces de Vie,* Centre Triades.

22 to 24 – Rudolf Steiner in *The World of the Senses and the World of the Spirit,* Hanover, 27 December, 1911 – 1 January, 1912, Lecture 2.

25 – In this chapter the information on iron is from W. Pelikan in *The Secret of Metals.*

CHAPTER 4

SUN PROCESS

The circulation of perceptions
Access to inner perception (insight)

Preamble: The Sun as a carrier of influences

In our Solar System the Sun is called a star because it emits energetic rays. Other bodies are called planets and reflect these sun rays in their elliptical dance around it. These planets have satellites (moons) that also reflect the sun rays. With our senses we perceive the sun ray as light that reveals space, colour and heat. Heat is the maestro of ceremonies in the changing states of matter. It is primarily heat that dictates whether a substance is solid, liquid or gaseous. With the rhythms of day and night, summer and winter caused by celestial movements, we receive varying amounts of heat and light from the Sun. The Sun's heat has the effect of lifting the air with its content of water and dust carrying the essence of an area, its fragrance and waste. The warm air going up invites a flow of air coming from cooler areas. Wind is born and so are clouds where the lifting water forms around the lifting dust (mineral or organic). This rising water creates fluffy cumulus clouds at a low level, and more evanescent cirrus at a higher level (see Note 1).

Note 1—Chemtrails

In the last few decades a new type of cloud has appeared: a long trail coming out of an airplane which doesn't disappear but expands in space resulting in a cloud bank that lowers the temperature for the next few days. These chemical trails or chemtrails are formed of nanoparticles of metallic dust (aluminium, barium and strontium) which fall over the Earth and sea. This is designed to create an artificial parasol to deflect the light and heat of the Sun—an attempt to control the weather. But, in doing so, it heats up the circumpolar jet streams and makes them faster and more unpredictable. The whole planet has become a lab where sorcerers' apprentices are experimenting. Life on Earth was never exposed to so much of these free metals. Strontium and Barium, sitting just below magnesium and calcium in the Periodic Table, have the same reactivity. Magnesium and Calcium are two essential metals for many life processes of living creatures. A sudden increase of Strontium and Barium can have unexpected consequences and disturb the fragile balance of life on the Earth and in the oceans.

This simple observation helps us to see heat as the generator of the circulation of air around the globe, from gentle breezes to ferocious hurricanes. High in the atmosphere we have powerful jet stream movements running around the poles.

Heat also activates powerful river currents (Gulf Stream) in the seas and oceans bringing a shake-up of influences between the equator and the poles. These air and water circuits in the northern hemisphere are anti-clockwise, and clockwise in the southern hemisphere.

The more heat there is the more water evaporates from the ocean and land. Even the Sahara, where the groundwater is deep underground, water evaporates all the time. The intense heat sucks out water and minerals through various strata and, on the surface, water evaporates leaving behind crystalline sand roses.

Heat generates circulation. In cold-blooded animals, the decrease of heat in winter forces the blood flow to slow down and the creature to hibernate. In animals, blood and nerves need warmth to function. This is true for plants as well, with the approach of spring and its increased warmth, sap starts to flow and buds will grow and open.

Sunlight reaches us either directly or is reflected by the Moon and planets. Steiner described our Sun as a black hole connecting us with 'counter-space' (the spiritual world).

> [The Sun] is a vacuum that exerts suction...The fine etheric structure of the universe, which is also spiritual, is continuously sucked in by the Sun as nourishment.
>
> RUDOLF STEINER (1)

Some cultures have similar concepts. Papua New Guineans, for instance, see the night sky as a canvas with holes in it to let the spirit world in.

Heat brings about metamorphic change—when it penetrates the elements of the Periodic Table matter is transformed into solid, liquid or gas. The hotter it is the more a substance tends towards gas, submitting itself to expansion and levity. In plants their essential oils, full of hydrogen, invade the air. A decrease of heat induces liquid and solid states that tend towards gravity.

The threeness of the Sun

Our Sun constantly rays down to Earth the influences of the star systems (the twelve constellations of the zodiac, each in turn containing their own radiating suns). Our Sun *light* holds the formative architectural blueprint of these stars. We live in the dynamic clock of the Universe and these supra-earthly forces bathe the Earth in their pulsed rhythms.

We are on the move inside a Solar System nested in the gigantic Milky Way galaxy that itself travels at 500,000 kilometres an hour towards the constellation of Hercules. All natural earthly manifestations have dynamic rhythmic systems of motion reaching a multitude of fulcrum points of equilibrium that are favourable for *life* in the dense world. In his 1979 book, *Gaia: A New Look at Life on Earth*, British scientist, James Lovelock (1919 –) is quite eloquent about it.

We perceive the Sun and the Moon as having the same size even though the Sun has 400 times the diameter of the Moon. The Sun has a diameter 400 of the Moon (approximately 1,400,000km against 3,479km) but is also 400 times further away (approximately 150,000,000km against 373,730km)! Coincidence?

There seems to be so many parameters present together in the right way at the right distance for life to flourish. The Earth is like a uterus for life expression leading to self-conscious being. In this coherent wisdom of the world, there is pouring *love*. Love is not yet an organizing force inside human societies even if we can perceive its presence throughout history. Steiner continually reiterated the mission of humankind on Earth: to create a cosmos of love by overcoming our animality.

Sun process: The circulation of outer perceptions and the access to inner perception (insight)

A. Life of circulation—distribution of influences
B. Heart and its landscape:
   blood and vessels, small intestine
C. Psychic influence: SHEN + reactivity
D. Metal: gold
E. Planetary seal
F. Summary of the heart landscape
G. For the health of this landscape

A. Life of circulation – distribution of influences

If, with the Mars Process (pictorial life), our consciousness develops pictures that form the basis of our psychic world, these pictures don't stop there.

> ...the pictures that are inhaled [Mars—life of breathing] are now spread through the whole organism through the circulation [and become formative] ... that these pictures then really become the whole inner organization is the work of the circulatory life.
>
> RUDOLF STEINER (2)

Circulation starts very early in the embryo. Some sort of cylindrical, muscular, elastic structures start a unique networking system typical for each species. This dynamic capillary system lays the framework for what is coming into manifestation. The capillaries are the first vessels to be created and, with the blood, start their networking matrix around the fifteenth day from what is called in histology the Islets of Pander and Wolff in the embryo. Already, from the third week we have the beginning of the formation of a two-chamber heart. This primitive heart is not there to pump blood but to regulate a circulatory pulse that is already generated by the muscular vessels. The lymphatic vessels will start to appear in the fifth week, born out of the intimacy of the newly formed organs. It is around these pulsating vessels (heart landscape) that the other four dynamic systems of organs and tissues (spleen, lung, kidney and liver landscape) will progressively form. Whatever the mother experiences, will directly impact on organ formation in the embryo, right from this beginning.

Nevertheless 'seeing the inner organization as solid organs with defined contours and position is a very small portion of man's organization' (3). It is tempting for the mind to think in this realm of clearly outlined parts, everything takes place in a mechanical way.

'It is more accurate to say that man is a column of liquids' (3) in movement where organs are floating, constantly destroyed and rebuilt while accomplishing their dynamic functions for the whole. Only the form/function seems to have a certain permanency while matter moves in and out.

Being the only tissue flowing in and out of the intimacy of our organs, the blood stream receives new impulses each time it passes through them. For instance, the blood will contract when passing through the lungs or kidneys by losing heat, water, gases, etc., whereas it will expand passing through the liver or heart by gaining heat, new substances and subtle impulses.

> Here the etheric body is the driving agent that mixes or separates the fluids, and brings about the processes of organic chemistry in man.
>
> RUDOLF STEINER (3)

The pulsating blood carries a summary of the whole internal environment. When entering an organ, this organ 'knows' immediately what is going on in all the other parts of the body. The blood is not just a carrier of food and waste; organs change the blood stream and constantly secrete hormonal messages to other organs to regulate the internal environment. There is a permanent dialogue between blood and organs. We know that our emotional reactivity will reverberate on the blood flow (blushing) and the biochemistry of our internal system of organs (psycho-somatic).

> There exist, then, inside our organism some processes similar to crystallization of salt and some others equivalent to the colloidal state and others more akin to thermo-genesis with a strong connection with our conscious life.
>
> RUDOLF STEINER (4)

Our soul activities of thinking, feeling and willing always have an impact on the way various liquids behave throughout our bodies.

> If we look at the blood which is the most active and subtle part of ourselves, we can observe salification (crystallization—when we think) as well as densification of liquid (gel/colloid—when we feel) and thermal processes (dissolution—when we move).
>
> RUDOLF STEINER (4)

This is happening in all organs of the body too. What we feel, think and do has a very direct impact on our health and wellbeing.

B. Heart and its landscape

The heart

The heart ideogram is like a flower. The two outer lines like petals protect the two inner lines delineating an open inner sanctum. At the bottom a stem indicates a link with a bigger ensemble through the vena cava and aorta. The ideogram also shows the envelope of the heart (pericardium).

Nowhere else in the body is the blood shaken more than in the systolic contractions of the heart. This is the YANG expansion nature of the heart (see Note 2 on YIN/YANG).

Note 2—YIN/YANG

In Chinese tradition, the concept of yin and yang is more complex than simply female/male or light/dark—YIN doesn't oppose YANG. The YANG day doesn't mean that the YIN darkness of the night is not there. The YANG light ether of the Sun rays might bring fertilizing formative forces from the stars during the day, but the YIN star background of the night is still there, it is simply too bright to see them. YANG as a directional force of transformation always manifests on the background of YIN as a passive, ever-present listener. Nothing is YIN or YANG by itself. They represent the basic duality of the dense world.

This succession of the blood in the heart creates millions of vortices. The shape and movement of the vortex has some mysterious properties in Nature, one of which is the ability to record information into the microstructure of water. Could the heart's movement be recording information about the blood's journey through the body and each organ? This is what the vortex does: it is a kind of ear/transducer/pencil.

To put a mathematic formula on the curves of a vortex we need the concept of infinity. It is part of a family of curves like the egg or bud shapes. Without being homeopathy as such, it is obvious that a dilution/succussion rhythm happens continually in us and the heart—kidneys are at the centre of this activity. Even the heart's continuous tendon has a vortex shape. (See two pictures: moving vortex + heart tendon.)

Figure 1: The movement of water spiralling around a vortex. From *Sensitive Chaos* by Theodor Schwenk.

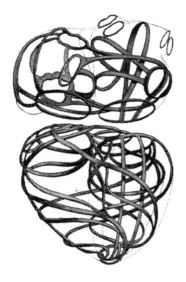

Figure 2: The tendons of the heart. Part of this picture (left ventricle) is shown in *Sensitive Chaos* and comes from a German book by Benninghoff, 1925.

To give you an idea of size, a person's heart is usually as big as their fist. The heart also has its own sensorial and motor brain. The sinoatrial node senses the flow of blood entering in the right atrium from the vena cava and initiates a contraction of the two atria at the same time. Then the atria-ventricular node is stimulated, provoking the contraction of the two ventricles at the same time. Then there is a pause. The atria contract first, and then the ventricles. These movements prompt the blue blood (more CO_2)

to go towards the lungs to gain more oxygen, and the red blood (more O2) through the aorta flows towards the rest of the body.

Consequently, the heart is not a simple pump but a complex organ that responds to the blood flow and adjusts to it. In doing this the heart emits a magnetic field beyond the thorax, stronger even than the brain's activity.

It is more accurate to say that our soul life moves the blood when we are awake and the blood moves the heart when asleep. Any emotional reaction has an immediate impact on breathing, circulation and the smooth muscle of our internal organs. With intense fear the blood withdraws from the skin whereas shame can make us blush.

The muscles of the heart are very different to the rest of our muscular structure. Each of the cells of our skeletal muscle are elongated multi-nucleated cells wrapped individually. Because of that a nerve ending must touch each of them. The H-type muscular cells of the heart muscle touch one another in the two atria. The muscular cells of the two ventricles don't touch the atrial cells and contract after the atria cells. It was difficult in the past to perceive these sensorial and motor systems because they are not made of conventional nerve but specialized muscular cells.

In the heart the blood undergoes its maximum expansion: nowhere else will the blood be shaken so strongly.

As the orchestra conductor of our inner rhythm, the heart landscape is an open system integrating various influences from food, air, climate or impulses coming from our psyche. It is the main organ of self-consciousness, not the brain. The brain is essential for self-knowledge but self-realization is the matter of the heart. From intention to individual achievement the warmth ether of the heart is made manifest.

The Greek Element Fire is predominant in this landscape

Heat state and warmth ether form a polarity. Heat is not considered a state of matter in science but only part of the electro-magnetic phenomenon in the huge section of the spectrum called infrared.

(See Note 3 on infrared and insects.) Nevertheless heat is still at the forefront of the theory about the origin of the Universe. If at zero degree Kelvin (minus 273 centigrade) we have a condition of matter with no heat at all, on the upscale of the thermometer we meet infinite heat. There is no maximum temperature. This state is called the Big Bang where an infinitely small, dense, hot point outside space-time starts to expand in the void. In *Occult Science* Steiner also described the beginning of the Solar System as a state where only heat and warmth ether existed, where time begins. He called it Old Saturn.

Note 3—The insect world in danger [19]

Aerials capture radio, T.V. and microwave frequencies and receive information of all kinds. Aerial and antennae forms and frequencies are a dynamic couple. Most species of Arthropoda, such as insects, have antennae of various kinds. Each insect species, which represent more then 90% of all animal species, has its own type of antenna—but what for?

The English astronomer, John Herschel (1792 – 1871) established the existence of invisible light. This part of the spectrum between red and microwave is infrared or heat. This area of the electro-magnetic spectrum is huge, encompassing 17 octaves between the colour red and microwave frequencies. A lot of primitive life forms have eyes that can capture aspects of the infrared spectrum in the same way as bees can perceive ultraviolet.

The American entomologist, Philip S. Callahan (1923 –) developed the idea that insect antennae are functional electro-magnetic aerials while working in Ireland as a tele-communication engineer in World War 2. He was intrigued by the strange cylindrical ancient towers in Ireland and saw them as resonators of cosmic forces for the fertility of the land around. He worked with the insight that tubular structures of all kinds (e.g. chimes) are propagators of sound, pulsed vibratory motions and other subtle influences from the cosmos. Archaeologists are still baffled by these ancient towers—there are at least 65 of them across Ireland and it is still unclear when and why they were built. They are monuments of an ancient knowledge.

He has espoused a mechanism of insect olfaction in which the antennae act as di-electric waveguides in detecting specific wavelengths of infrared radiations emitted by excited free-floating odorant molecules (pheromones). For him, the micro-millimetre microscopic coverings (sensilla) of their antennae could be enough to tap into this vast portion of the spectrum.

The ever-present infrared radiations stimulate gas molecules (already with a tendency to expand) to oscillate at a specific infrared frequency. This system informs an insect species about distance, direction, mating, navigation, communication. His experiments on insect antennae point to a connection between chemistry and electro-magnetic effects.

In the last few decades entomologists have observed a significant decrease in the insect population in Europe. This decrease happened at the same time as the increase of microwave radiations for telecommunication purposes. In order for these mini mobile computers with a phone facility to operate 24/7, we need to enormously increase the signal. This increase of microwaves (which is close to the infrared bands) effectively 'heats' this air. And this increase needs to be looked at as far as the life of insects is concerned. Of course other factors such as new types of insecticides must also play a part.

An intense heat state (fire) will destroy shapes and forms and make them disappear. Heat is also the changing agent for the elements to go from solid, liquid and gas according to their heat content. The heat state brings levity, expands and penetrates the other three states of matter. It can't be imprisoned. Rays from the sun have heat and light, but in interstellar space it is dark and cold. To be revealed to our senses they need to interact with the other states of matter i.e. our atmosphere or our senses. Heat is also created in association with pressure. Impose pressure on solid crystalline matter and not only is heat produced but also a piezoelectric pulse.

The warmth ether ripens and matures life. It invites seeds to unfold their project. The ideogram FIRE reveals aspects of this warmth ether. FIRE means expansion, a movement of intensification of exchange between an inside and an outside. As an organized force at the origin of a human being, FIRE prompts a consciousness of the whole. Its radiant gesture creates networks, such as blood vessels linking the intimacy of each organ within the whole. This is an aspect of what the heart landscape warmth ether is all about.

In the *Warmth Course,* (1 March to 14 March, 1920) Steiner writes:

> We have to consider will as akin to heat—as the transformative forces of outer objects are akin to mental activity [the emergence of pictures out of sensorial perceptions]. ...Heat must therefore be looked upon as will, or we may say that we experience the being of heat in our will.

Through our strong heartbeats the oscillations of diluted substances are stabilized in the water micro-structure of the blood and distributed as energizing forces. The Master of the Heart (as an etheric organ) assists in the distribution of our personalized liquid light in the whole body.

Humans as self-conscious beings, can't perceive this ether but can transform their internal heat state into compassion, love, empathy. Through the heart (site of our self-consciousness) we can go from heat state to warmth ether. The heart is a dwelling for the Spirit who keeps us in communication with the spiritual dimension through insightful light-bulb moments (imagination, inspiration, intuition). Warmth ether/Heat state is the first manifested substance of love in the world of density.

On January 2, 1924 at the beginning of a Christmas course, Steiner stated that the Greek Fire Element is the instrument that the 'I AM' uses to penetrate the whole organism:

> It is through the warmth ether that the psychic life rings out on the organs.

Teilhard de Chardin (1881 – 1955), Jesuit palaeontologist, helped us realize, like many other philosophers, that humankind's expression is an unfinished business in progress. In *The Phenomenon of Man* he reminded us that 'some day, when we have mastered the wind, the tides and gravity, we will harness the energies of love. Then, for a second time in the history of the world, man will have discovered fire.'

The blood and its vessels

The blood, this liquid tissue, travels in a complex vascular system that has its own elasticity and muscular activity. If there is no food to digest, the blood flow slows down in the digestive system. As soon as food comes in then the valves reopen. When we are asleep our muscles receive only a little bit of blood for maintenance but when we run the valves are completely open for our muscles to receive lots of blood. The blood vessels, with their smooth muscles, regulate the flow by responding to hormones (prostaglandins/tissue hormones) and the influx of the autonomic nervous system that rules the internal environment. Some organs, such as the heart, brain and kidneys don't have valves—the blood flow is continuous in these areas.

Like the axons of the nerves and the skeletal muscles, the blood vessels are also made of three layers. The endothelium is composed of one cell layer. The blood travels in this layer in all the veins and arteries. Then we have a second layer, in veins and arteries, made of elastic tissue + smooth muscles that insure vasoconstriction or dilation when it is needed. The whole is wrapped within a denser third layer.

From the heart the arteries spread the red (oxygenated) blood into smaller conduits. It is at a capillary level in the intimacy of each corner of the body that the blood starts to exchange with the cells of organs. At that level there is only one layer of cells left (endothelium) carrying the blood. Except for the amoeba-like lymphocytes, only what is soluble can go in and out. Then the blood vessels start to get bigger on their way back to the heart and form a kind of venous pulsing reservoir that can hold up to 70% of the blood—it is called blue blood (carbon dioxide rich) at this stage.

In the exchange at a cellular level, more water stays in the tissues. This gives rise to another circulation: the lymphatic system. Like a hoover, these muscular vessels, with their one-way valves, suck in any compounds (bacteria, dead cells) that couldn't go into the blood stream. It is an inner digestive system that goes through digestive organs (lymphatic ganglions) before pouring its cleaned lymph into the vena cava just before the blue blood enters the heart. The lymph circulation is part of the defence of the territory (immunity) under the governance of the liver landscape.

In the micro-cosmos of our body, the five seasonal HUA (see Preamble in Chapters 2 and 3) of expansion and contraction operate much faster. We can observe this in the blood, the only liquid tissue that goes into the intimacy of each organ. Blood flow is constantly submitted to these movements every minute of our life according to the organ it flows through. By travelling into organs the blood will acquire and maintain a multitude of fulcrum points of balance, such as a Ph around 7.4, a temperature around 38 degrees centigrade and a multitude of other parameters like concentration of sugar, calcium etc...

Our blood vessels contain 4 to 6 litres of this viscous liquid. Our heart, on average, receives from the vena cava and gives to the aorta 5.25 litres a minute. These litres flow through 100,000 km of vessels every day!

Secretion and the I consciousness

> The faculty to inscribe something on the blood [coming from sense impressions], to produce an effect relies only on these interactions between the nerves and the blood circulation.
>
> RUDOLF STEINER (5)

Light, sound, touch, smell and taste, entering us, bear subtle formative impulses. Bring rock music to a milking parlour and the production of milk will decrease. The opposite will happen with a Mozart symphony. Everything entering through our senses from outside is written in the blood as if it were a tablet. The activity of our inner organs is also influencing the blood.

Our organs can be seen as five landscapes (connected with the main organs: heart, spleen, lungs, kidneys and liver) reflecting the daily and seasonal rhythms of Nature. Like the Sun outside, the heart/blood stream is central because it interconnects all the other organs into a functioning circulatory unity. This system of pulsing circulation is, in essence, an emanation of the 'I'. The heart/blood stream is impacted by outside influences through food, air and perceptions and also by our other inner landscapes as they form their own response to outside influences by secreting substances that constantly transform the blood stream with their activities.

Clear perceptions of the outside through the central nervous system (CNS) and dim perceptions of the inside through the autonomic nervous system (ANS) are attributes of the life of the psyche, whereas the circulatory system, extremely sensitive to the secretion of the five dynamic landscapes, is an essential instrument for the building of the soma.

> The blood stream is the most easily influenced and mobile [landscape], and the least capable of stability, open completely to the conscious Self.
>
> RUDOLF STEINER (6)

The blood couldn't be the instrument of the I if it was able to crisscross our organism without any change. Man depends on the constant changes that the blood undergoes. It is modified all the time and renews itself, so that Man is not only possessing an I, but he can experience it consciously with the help of a sensitive instrument (blood).

RUDOLF STEINER (7)

These five landscapes absorb, separate, divide, transform and secrete what is received in parts that are useful and others that need to be eliminated. It is as though the diverse substances meet a resistance when entering an organ and need to be transformed. Without the resistance of the organs to the substances:

Man wouldn't be able to have an experience of himself. (8)

Small intestine

Just as the heart is at the centre of the thorax surrounded by the lungs, the small intestine is at the centre of the abdomen surrounded by the large intestine. In the movement of liquid light flowing in the meridians the heart and the small intestine are connected. In Chinese physiology the small intestine is the workshop organ of the heart. This is a long (around three to six metres) tubular muscular elastic tube where the white milk (intestinal chyme) of our daily meals is made and absorbed. It has its own sensory/motor activities that generate peristaltic beats responding to the food coming in and directing the flow towards the large intestine. All sorts of soul states can affect the peristaltism through the autonomic nervous system and hormonal release. The fight-or-flight response to stressful situations can seriously impair the digestion of food because the blood withdraws from this system.

What separates the chyme from the blood/lymph currents is one layer of cells constantly renewing itself—an inner skin highly glandular like all epithelium tissues. This single layer is supported by an elastic and muscular tissue ensuring a good blend and movement towards the large intestine. When active the small intestine produces two litres of alkaline liquid (Ph 7.4) consisting of mucus plus all kinds of enzymes. Digestion and absorption happen mainly here. This organ is highly folded and its interior is full of villi (fingers). Each cell of these villi, in touch with the chyme, extends multiple micro-villi that vastly expand its effective surface, providing a surface area the size of a tennis court in a very compact space.

C. Psychic influence: SHEN

Both heat in Nature and the heart landscape in us initiate circulatory movements. This activity reverberates in the psychic entity of the heart as a circulation between the creator and the created. In many ancient Chinese texts SHEN is discussed.

> In this context Shen and all the other four creative psychic entities of the inner landscapes (YI, P'O, ZHI, HUN) are speculative images (not concepts) of 'pure action' that can't be perceived directly.
>
> JEAN-MARC EYSSALET (9)

One aspect of the ideogram SHEN represents the heaven with its luminaries that are signs that inform humans about transcendental things. Cosmic bodies are our ciphers of the celestial creative plan. The other part of the ideogram shows two hands climbing a vertical axis. The self-conscious human being is seen here as a hyphen between the formative forces raining down and their realization.

With Shen we are talking about a cosmic conjunction between the formative principle (emanation of the celestial star system) and the concrete physical form. Between this couple there is a constant dialogue flowing in a vertical axis and centring in a human being.

As a summary we can say that this ideogram shows the heart to be an interface between heaven and earth. SHEN, an I AM, pre-exists the moment of conception and allows the passage from the formless to the formed or concrete. SHEN allows the mind to access imagination, inspiration and intuition. The physical heart is a dwelling for SHEN which spreads through the warmth of the blood.

It is interesting to notice that people living with the heart of another person undergo some psychic changes in their habits and preferences. A few books have been written about it. The memoir *A Change of Heart* (1997) by American author Claire Sylvia is quite eloquent about it. It seems as if they pick up some memory aspects of the donor. These facts tend to confirm the assertion that organs are not only functional but they contribute to our psychic life and store deep psychic tendencies. Each of the five landscapes described here holds a basic psychic tendency allowing our soul activities to unfold. These tendencies are called creative spirits in the old Chinese texts. The SHEN of the heart landscape is central to our whole organization, as the king is to his kingdom. Being responsible right at the beginning of the embryonic life in the organization of the physical territory (networking of blood vessels/blood), at a psychic level the heart region allows our spirit to continue to be in touch with the spiritual world. It is often through insights (inner perceptions) that our creativity unfolds.

The heart is the centre for global intuitive intelligence. Unlike the mind, SHEN has no judgemental attitudes, dogmatism or competition. The 'I' dwelling in the heart and spreading in the warmth of the blood stream needs silence to hear the spiritual dimension.

Inner and outer perceptions feed the thinking activity all the time. In both the intentional 'I', must be there. We can walk through a forest path full of sounds and scents and perceive nothing if the mind is focused on an inner problem; this can block our awareness of outer stimuli. Our senses are open but if the light of SHEN, its intentionality to perceive, is not there, then there is no conscious perception. In the same way, if we perceive too much too fast—e.g. hours of surfing the internet—the 'I' doesn't have enough inner silence to digest things and gets a sort of sensory information overload, a data bulimia, if you will.

When science and technology try to replicate human intelligence with ever more sophisticated machines and artificial intelligence, there is confusion between the meaning of intelligence and consciousness. Artificial Intelligence can have an advanced intelligence programmed by a conscious human being. The processing of data and mathematic calculations, to mention just two, can be done much faster as a kind of replica of our rational intelligence. Many operations in the construction of cars are done by robots mimicking our craftsman intelligence. We can even program computers to simulate artistic activities. But they can't have inner perceptions or contact with the spiritual dimension of the Universe. Depending on the morality and skill of their human programmers, robots can act morally or not.

Primal Emotion

As the heart gives the blood its full expansion, so does the emotion of excitement we share with the animals. Facing pleasant events (such as the prospect of a holiday) this emotion seems to open new possibilities of expression in the present and future. Observe a dog anticipating a walk or a child being promised a weekend of boating. Like any primal emotion, it can become an extreme feeling in us. Constant excitement or elation can be quite taxing for the heart.

The lesson of excitement is inner stability (serenity).

D. Metal related to the sun: gold

Gold in Nature

All the earthly processes that tend to eliminate the metallic state of existence ...through rust, weathering, oxidation, calcification, etc. are powerless to do all this to gold.

R. HAUSCHKA (10)

Gold is a kind of king and doesn't combine easily with other elements. One exception is liquid mercury which can dilute it but there is no chemical bond.

Paradoxically, although gold is rare and precious, it is widely prevalent in microscopic quantities everywhere [rock deposits as well as sea water]. It seems as if the Earth has a high dilution of that substance…Where found with other elements, gold stands like a rhythmically connecting principle between silica [quartz] and sulphur.

R. HAUSCHKA (11)

Gold is an excellent conductor of heat and electricity. While some other metals (lead, tin or quicksilver) lose all resistance to electric currents under rapid cooling and become 'super-conductive with liquid helium, gold does not let itself be altered thus by cold.' (12)

Gold can be flattened into a film less than a ten-thousandth of a millimetre thick. A wire almost 35 miles long can be made from a single ounce of gold.

A form in which the 'light aspect' of gold is especially manifest is the mirror, where the gold backing, almost wholly two-dimensional, most nearly approaches light. It is all lustre, transparent, thin as a breath, and at the same time all colour. To make the mirror, the metal is first vaporized. As a shining blue-green 'steam', it is a 'being of colour'. Out of this colouring it condenses to a golden film on the cold walls of the vessel in which it is vaporized. In this form it is very pure. It can be brought into this condition only by the hand of man.

WILHELM PELIKAN (13)

Of course, nowadays, most mirrors are backed with silver or other cheaper materials because gold is too expensive.

From external analogies it is assumed that the ancients saw in gold a representative of the Sun. But it was not merely a superficial way of analogies that considered the Sun something precious in the sky and gold something precious on Earth…[Modern man is apt to impute stupidity to the ancients.] When they looked at gold, with its self-possessed radiantly yellow colour and its modesty and dignity, they actually felt something related to man's entire blood circulation. Confronted with the quality of gold, they felt: I am within this, here I can feel myself. And by virtue of this feeling they understood the nature of what is Sun-like. They felt the kinship of the quality of gold with what came from the Sun and worked in the blood of man.

RUDOLF STEINER (14)

Gold in us

In minute doses gold is very useful for heart and circulation disorders.

Like the earth and sea, our body liquids have gold at a potency of five to nine decimals according to the part of the body. The cerebrospinal fluid close to the grey matter of the brain has low potency of gold and other minerals.

> Connected with the effect of gold on the circulation is an effect on the warmth organization. It is useful for chills, heat flashes, night sweats.
>
> RUDOLF STEINER (15)

When gold acts as oscillating activity in us it acts as a harmonizing substance. It represents the activity of the spirit being present in the heart as its dwelling place.

> In our observations of the inorganic world, we noted the position of gold between light and gravity; the blood, with the heart at its centre, lives in the body in a similar polar tension between light and air, and between weight and the forces of matter. Gold combines neither with silica nor with oxygen, but it penetrates quartz, which in man stimulates the sense activity, and it accompanies iron, which in man lies at the foundation of breathing.
>
> RUDOLF STEINER (16)

If we are serious about overcoming materialism, and we look for the creative spirituality behind all material objects, we must expect to find a definite differentiated spirituality behind every earthly substance and process. Having this clearly in mind, we will admit the validity of spiritual research as we admit the validity of scientific research (when observing only matter)... that gold, for example, is a basic mineral substance that received its essence from the sun itself.

RUDOLF STEINER (17)

E. Sun seal

The external line waves along like a seven-petalled expression that starts to sub-divide, by invagination, part of the internal environment. This 'gastrula' or involuted movement impacts on the shape of the middle line.

If the external line of the Mars seal has discontinuity suggesting pulsations, it is the middle line, here, that is not continuous. These middle lines form new vessels opening entirely the internal environment. They allow a free circulation between the centre and its periphery.

The centre is a cluster of seeds ready to spread through the tubules.

If the entry of impressions is pictorial for the consciousness (psyche) it is also formative for our organs (soma). These sensorial impressions, holding energies that impact on form, swarm all over the body through the blood stream: a world of continuous flow. It is the only seal that has no enclosed space—entirely opened to circulation.

F. Summary of the heart landscape [18]

Inner organic world
- Treasure organs: heart and Master of the Heart
- Workshop organ: small intestine and Triple Warmer
- Associated tissue: vascular systems as a matrix linking the intimacy of all organs
- Energy tendency: full expansion of structure
- Vitality of the distribution of the liquid light in meridians and liquids
- Dynamic of the blood and lymph circulation

At the skin level the inner world perceives, or insures the health of
- Flavour and texture: roasted meat, torrefaction (coffee). Fibrous food
- Body liquid: sweat
- Transformed skin: the colour of the face, the light of the eyes

In the psychic world
- Psychic instrument: SHEN as the source of global intuitive intelligence keeping us in touch with the spirit world. It is not because our perceptual organs are opened that we perceive consciously. The conscious presence in the heart (I AM) must have the intention to observe the outer world. When too busy in our psychic world (anxiety) we don't perceive consciously.
- Primal emotion: excitement
- Negative feelings: elation, restless
- Vocal expression: laughing
- The health of a perceptual organ: the tongue (called the bud of the heart by the ancient Chinese) for taste and speech.

G. For the health of this landscape

- Mastery over restless excitement, hatred, cruelty, egoism, impatience, apathy, hopelessness
- The search for equilibrium between hypo and hyper states in our emotional life.
- Because the heart expands the blood some bitter food is good as it contracts it.
- Extreme heat is hazardous—the heart is already a fiery organ.
- Be aware of palpitation, high blood pressure, chest pain—these are messages from the heart.
- Inner silence helps to ground our work with insights.
- A short siesta favours intestinal assimilation.
- Eat in good relaxed company.
- Cultivate tranquility and gentleness.
- Exercise that stimulates the circulation is good for blood pressure.

References

1 – Rudolf Steiner in discussions with the Goetheanum's workmen, 18 Sept., 1924, in *From Beetroot to Buddhism*, Rudolf Steiner Press, 1999. W. Sucher in *Lectures to Experimental Circle at Peredur*, Lect. 2, 10 Jan., 1956.
Rudolf Steiner in *The Mystery of the Universe*, Lect. 3 (11 April 1920), 4 (16 April 1920), 15 (15 May, 1920).

2 – Rudolf Steiner in *Forming of Man through Cosmic Influences (Form, Life, Soul & Spirit)*, Dornach, 28 Oct. – 5 Nov, 1921. Translated by M. Cotterell.

3 – Rudolf Steiner, *The Origin of Natural Science*, Dornach, 3 Jan., 1923.

4 – Rudolf Steiner in *Occult Physiology*, 27 March, 1911.

5 – Rudolf Steiner, *Occult Physiology* (p. 60).

6 – Idem.

7 – Idem.

8 – Idem.

9 – Jean-Marc Eyssalet in *Shen ou L'instant créateur*.

10 – R. Hauschka in *The Nature of Substance*.

11 – Ibid.

12 – Wilhelm Pelikan, *The Secrets of Metals*.

13 – Ibid.

14 – Ibid. quoted from Rudolf Steiner in *Initiate Consciousness*.

15 – Ibid.

16 – Ibid.

17 – Ibid.

18 – Jean-Marc Eyssalet in *Les Cinq Chemins du Clair and de l'Obscur*, Trédaniel.

19 – The insects' antennae are tuned to receive messages in the infrared spectrum with its 17 octaves of possibility....Philip S. Callahan in *Tuning into Nature*, 1974 and *Exploring the Spectrum*, 1994.

Chapter 5
MERCURY PROCESS

From pictorial images (psyche)
to material organs (soma)

Preamble: What is an organ?

The three-ness of organ formation

Modern physiology defines an organ as an assemblage of tissues and has a good understanding of their complex structures and bio-chemical functions. The research continues, however, as organs haven't revealed all their secrets. Materialistic scientists are still in awe at the embryonic emergence of this harmonious complex assemblage.

At the physical level, we can identify separate organs that have a special shape, size, location, colour, texture. Through research we constantly identify new aspects of their function inside the whole. Each organ, for instance, will transform the blood and dialogue in a special way with the brain and other organs through hormones.

A living body is made of layer upon layer of tissue. These tissues generate envelopes—facias (surfaces)—where the organs will develop their own niche in order to work and interrelate.

> ...it is through the physical that we see the etheric form; but it is the etheric form which we really see and the physical form is only the means by which we can see the etheric.
>
> RUDOLF STEINER (1)

Each organ develops its own *sensory/motor network* in relation with its *metabolic processes* with *a unique rhythm*. All the organs are in constant dialogue with the whole through three moving matrices: the flow of bio-electricity through the nerves, the pulsing blood-lymph circulation through the network of vessels and the 24-hour 'liquid light' movement through the meridians.

Every living creature has this three-ness. So it is for each organ too. An organ is a living entity in action, an intelligence, a vector of activity that wants to manifest and have a conversation with the whole. Scientists have long known that the large intestine has millions of neurons, for instance. Known as the Enteric Nervous System, it is recognized as being autonomous and reacting independently from the brain. Because organs have neural connections, specific pulses and metabolic secretions, they reveal to us their astral nature. It is called astral because we internalize the formative forces of the 'moving stars' (the planets). Ancient astronomers observed that some stars have a loopy pathway around the Earth from a geo-centric point of view and gave them organic and psychic functions.

With their capacity to grow and renew themselves, organs show their etheric nature. Because of their activities, organ systems reverberate into our soul as psychic tools with emotional reactivity. From the building of the soma the I AM will build its unique psychic world. A drawing by Steiner in *Occult Physiology* shows well these four constituents. (Figure 1)

Organ summary

At the centre we have an organ.

This dark dense shape is covered with a grid. These lines of force represent the bi-dimensional aspect of the etheric world made of moving lines and surfaces. This is the morphic field of the organ in constant

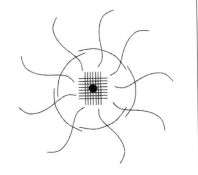

Figure 1: Organ and supersensible members from a Steiner's sketch (*Occult Physiology*)

formation. It is inside this field that stem cells will differentiate using a fraction of the genes to produce organs. The Earth, nested inside a living Solar System, is surrounded by the morphic fields of the planets that reverberate in us as organ systems (soma).

The wavy lines represent two things: the somato-psychic and the psycho-somatic. The progressive emergence of the soma is the basis for the psychic world to develop over a few decades. It gives us the reactivity we share with animals. Once in place this psychic world, in turn, also impacts on the soma.

The whole drawing is surrounded by curved lines forming a permeable sphere open to the outside world and protecting this inner sanctum. It symbolizes the Spirit as a conscious centre of incarnation.

When we observe a machine or a house, a human-made object, we are aware of a human creative intelligence. When it's completed, the builders are not *à l'oeuvre* anymore. They are behind the construction, in the past. With living creatures, the intelligent activity behind the form is always there and there is a constant rebuilding process *à l'oeuvre*. The flow of air and food is needed to renew us all the time.

Nevertheless, healthy organic life is hidden from our consciousness. The whole interior is governed by the autonomic nervous system (ANS) with its many little brains of grey matter peppered all over the thorax and abdomen. The mission of the ANS is to synchronize the organs between the fatigue due to the use of our soul faculties with a period night-time recovery.

Embryology

If we want to have an understanding of where, when and how organs emerge in us we need to observe their appearance and movement in the embryo. Here we are faced with more questions than answers. The original cells coming from the meeting of a sperm and ovule are called stem cells or mesenchyme. These cells, which are still dormant in our adult connective tissue, reproduce in the embryo to form the tissues—the surfaces. Stem cells become specialized to form organs according to special 'loci'. It was French biologist Alexis Carrel (1873 – 1944), in his study of chicken embryos in the 1930s, who first observed the development of these cells. When they became a specific organ or tissues in the embryo, Carrel moved some of these differentiated cells to somewhere else in the embryo. These stem cells then underwent a de-differentiation to become specialized in the new organ.

The whole dialogue starts when the ectoderm tissue (future skin) invaginates/involutes inside to form a neural tube where the central nervous system will emerge. Very soon the somites (mesoblasts) glue to this tube to form 44 pairs. It is here that the dance starts. Right at the beginning one of the basis for organ formation (somites) is intimately associated with the start of the spinal cord in the neural tube. Nothing happens randomly (see Note 1 with Figures 2 A and B).

Note 1—Cell movements in the embryo

After fertilization, continuous cell division produces a package of cells (morula) that becomes a hollow sphere (blastula). Then something totally unexpected happens. Cells in an area of that sphere start to differentiate and move inwards (invagination). It is also known as gastrulation and is the start of a multi-layered and multi-cavity organism. Primitive animals, such as sponges, jellyfish and medusae, for instance, don't reach this level of development. Their existence is made of two layers: one sensitive skin facing outside (ectoderm) and another internal skin digesting food (endoderm). With gastrulation, starting the third week, the mesoderm makes the embryo a tri-laminar organism, each layer developing in harmony with the others.

The formation of the neural tube is a good example of gastrulation. (Figure 2 A) An area of the ectoderm (1) undergoes an inward migration of cells following a cartilaginous ruler (the notochord (2)). The remnant of this notochord (nucleus pulposae) is still present inside the cartilaginous disc between the vertebrae. There is a desire in this gesture to form a cavity (inner sanctum) where an exceptional organ can appear. In this instance a neural tube is formed where vertebrae and the neural cord develop. This invagination of cells that creates an inner cavity is very common in the embryo and gives rise very early to the pleuroperitonial cavity.

Figure 2A: Gastrulation of the skin in the embryo

Another cell movement is inversion. At the head end of the embryo the vertebrae metamorphose into the cranium bones. In this cavity the neural cord will develop into a bud that will give rise to the various stages of brain formation. At the entrance to the brain there is an inversion of nerves where the right side of our body relates with the left side of the brain and vice versa. In the neural cord the grey matter (butterfly shape of neuronal cells) is surrounded by white matter (axons of the neuronal cells). In the brain the situation is partially reversed: the grey matter surrounds the white matter at the surface of the hemispheres.

In the formation of the eye (Figure 2 B) we witness a gastrulation/inversion phenomenon. The brain vesicle undergoes an exvagination that becomes a cup shape. At the bottom of that cup the retina appears. The retina is a tissue that reacts with light. In response to this inward movement the ectoderm invaginates to meet this cup and forms the lens. The lens is a crystalloid transparent protein set of fibres made of successive elastic layers like an onion. An inside-out gesture of cells to perceive the light meets an outside-in gesture providing the crystalline lens for the retina to receive the light. We actually meet a similar structure in the relation between the bladder and the kidney (see glomerular capsule, Venus Chapter, Figure 2 B).

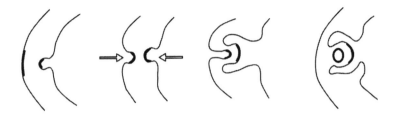

Figure 2 B: Formation of the eyes by inversion of the brain vesicle (retina) meeting a gastrulation of the skin (lens)

A third cell movement is a bit more elusive: some stem cells become free from their original membranes and start to travel in the various cavities, becoming tissue here and organ there. We know that each cell in our body contains the complete genetic code. What we don't know is how, in a specific locus, a cell will use only a fraction of its genes to produce proteins. It is here that the notion of morphic field is an interesting hypothesis. The observation is clear: a locus determines gene differentiation.

In a strange choreography, the somites split into several layers—some glue to other somites, others migrate to the right place. Sometimes only one part of the somite travels. All these somites will give rise to most of the axial skeleton (vertebrae) plus its muscles, the skin and various tissues such as ligaments, tendons and facias, that allow the unification and separation of the organs. Each organ has a special function in the whole and encloses itself in a single or double serous membrane (pleura for the lungs, pericardium for the heart, periosteum for the bones, etc...).

By the end of the second month all the organs are more or less settled after their migratory dance. The primitive heart, one of the first organs to appear, forms outside the embryo and migrates to its final place before the formation of the thoracic cage. Primitive kidneys will grow and disappear while a new one will rise below the diaphragm. It is about this time that we call the embryo a foetus. And this foetus will undergo a growth process that will end about two decades later when the adult human being is fully grown.

This observation confirms the fact that a specific place in the embryo has a tremendous impact on cell differentiation leading towards the creation of a specific organ. This aspect of how the shape of living things are created is one of the greatest mysteries of modern biology. There is no good theory in mainstream biology to account for why we grow to be the shape that we are. We can imagine a field around an organ made of lines of forces which seems to have a specific impact on gene differentiation. After all, each of our cells carries the totality of the genetic material, but according to the locus each cell will use only a small portion of its DNA to produce specific proteins. So it seems a locus is an area in the embryo that can generate a form. The English embryologist Rupert Sheldrake called it (as did earlier vitalists) a morphogenetic field. The organs are the final result of 'a system of forces working behind the outer appearances'.

It seems that the material adapts itself to the immaterial.

RUDOLF STEINER (2)

And once the organ is formed, for the rest of our lives, this organ, in its materiality, will constantly dismantle and rebuild itself within that form. Facing this simple observable fact 'we can't look at an organ as a static form, but rather we should see it has a nodal point within a constant flow of coming into being and passing away again'. (3) Only the form/function of an organ has a relative permanency.

In the etheric body we see first the bearer of all life manifestation [seven metabolic processes]. The body doesn't succumb to the laws of physics and chemistry because of the etheric body. It allows the constant coming into existence and passing away of organs, tissues and cells.

RUDOLF STEINER (4)

We have seen that the outside perceptions reach the blood via the cerebrospinal system (CSS). The inside perceptions of our systems of organs reach the blood via the autonomic nervous system (ANS). The CSS allows the conscious perception of the outside world, whereas the ANS brings a dim, vague perception of what is going on inside us. The organs are, in a sense, our internal universe reflecting the activity of the planetary system we are living in.

Entelekheia* (entelechy)

Considering the nature of organs (physical, etheric and astral), there is a fourth element giving a direction to all the organs forming a species. Beside the physical substance organized around lines of force (blueprints), forming organ landscapes that give rise to a surge of astral reactivity (soul), there is an organizational principle or entelechy.

Entelekheia means *to be in a certain state of perfection within.* Here we have the idea of the Higher Self that guides the physical and psychic functioning of an organism. And this I AM is on its way towards more perfection.

The 'I AM' uses the soul faculties of the astral body that are generated by organ landscapes, while physical substances constantly flow in and out (etheric body).

The inner life of an animal is locked in the sphere of his organs. These organs are the masters of ceremony that the spirit [architect] has formed in order that their inner life [psyche] can unfold

---

Entelekheia, from: *en*—within, *tele*—perfection, and *ekhein*—to be in a certain state.

[according to the form/expression of its species]. ...Goethe said that the animal is instructed by its organs, but the human being has the power to instruct his own.

RUDOLF STEINER (5)

The Entelekheia or I Am as a will intention, has a drive to manifest inside a physical vehicle; externally, by following the blueprint of the architects (pulsing formative forces of the twelve constellations of the Milky Way) that generate the outer form; internally, by following the blueprint of the pulsing planetary spheres that give rise to organ systems and their metabolic processes. The building materials produced by the genetic material are trapped by the force lines of the morphic fields of organs. These organ systems provide the basic tools for the surge of the psyche. From this formation the soul, with its various faculties, starts to unfold. Newborn babies take a couple of decades to develop these various ways to apprehend the world (thinking, feeling and willing). The I Am then can use these various forms of intelligences to realize its destiny.

Mercury process: From pictorial images (psyche) to material organs (soma) – a constant search for hormonal balance

A. Life of metabolism—a flow of changes
B. Lung and its landscape: large intestine and the glandular epithelium
C. Psychic influence: PO + reactivity
D. Metal: mercury
E. Mercury seal
F. Summary of the lung landscape
G. For the health of this landscape

A. Life of metabolism – a flow of changes

When we want to build a house we take part of a forest (wood) or mountain (stone) as building material. We dismantle it. This is catabolism: the process inside our body in which complex substances are converted to simpler soluble, usable ones, i.e., a tree into a plank of wood. Using this wood or stone we build the house. We create something new. This is anabolism: the process by which our body creates the right compounds for repair and growth. Metabolism, meaning change, consists of both these processes. The entering perceptions of the outer world that build our psychic world also creates our soma, our physical body.

> These images that we breathe in are diffused in the whole body by the life of the circulation. This life of the circulation is in connection with the metabolism (Mercury Process) and it is there that the substance starts to integrate itself into the images [morphic field].
>
> RUDOLF STEINER (6)

The Mercury-nature presses the substance through the human organism into separate organs.

> The faculty to write down something on the blood, to produce an effect on it resides in the interaction of the nerve with the blood circulation. The cerebro-spinal system influences the blood when the outside world enters through our senses.
>
> RUDOLF STEINER (7)

> With the respiratory process, it is materially that we absorb the outer world. With the perception and—I mean here the total impressions that are coming from outside—we interiorize inside our organism a kind of spiritual respiratory process [intake of odour. flavour, light, sound, touch]. The process of perception adds itself to the respiratory process [ventilation] like a superior process.
>
> RUDOLF STEINER (8)

Two streams are constantly present in our make-up: one from food (digestion) and air (ventilation) responsible for our material structure (soma); the other one from perception (sensorial organs) responsible for the emergence of our psyche.

Embryology

> Everything that appears later, during the course of the evolution of any living creature, is laid down beforehand in the germinal plan. What I have here explained to you, as the complicated human organization, exists potentially in the germinal plan of the human being as it builds itself up, when once it is produced through the process of impregnation (fertilization). If we retrace the course, so to speak, from this fully formed man to the germinal plan, we are able to discover that inside this life-seed or germ complicated systems of organs in miniature, scarcely visible at first, even to microscopic examination, are present as the very first plan; present in such a way indeed, that the organs even at that time already reveal just how they are related to one another.
>
> RUDOLF STEINER (9)

Inside this growing ball of identical cells (mesenchyme or stem cells) the embryo will develop progressively surrounded by the external cover of trophoblasts on their way to become the placenta and various membranes. They are the successive internal skins linking and separating various cavities. After the start of the implantation of the embryo in the uterus membrane (a week after fertilization) there are, already, several skins delimiting cavities: amniotic, coelome (chorionic cavity), lecithocele (yolk sac). These separate pools of liquid feed the cells of the embryonic disc and are spaced where organs can expand.

A spectacular change emerges around the third week with the development of the embryonic disc from which all future organs will be formed. It is called gastrulation. The external cells (ectoblasts) will start to flow inward (invagination) following progressively a medio-dorsal line initiating our bi-lateral symmetry with the head/tail orientation. This movement will give rise to the mesoblast located between the ectoblast and the endoblast. These three layers of cells are at the origin of all the organs. This increase in complexity facilitates a better movement of liquids between the embryo and the mother because the blood vessels start their pulsed networking before the formation of the primitive heart. In other words the vessels appear before the heart.

At this stage, whatever the mother ingests including food, medication, sights, sounds, feelings and psychic activity will impact on this fragile creation.

First the germinal cell develops into two layers fed by the uterine membrane. Gastrulation provides a third tissue (mesoblast). Then various assemblies of tissues start the creation of organs in an orderly cavalcade, with the progressive nesting of the embryo in the uterine membrane.

This is possible because of the life of metabolism (metabole = change). In the carbohydrate architecture of plants, it is in the metabolic area of flower/seed that we extract most of our protein and oil. With the protein architecture of animals and humans, this is an ongoing activity with the liver at the forefront.

Enzymes* and co-factors

Just as humans make tools to transform our environment, our inner sanctum constantly creates thousands of enzymes to renew our protein architecture. Created by cells, the enzyme production depends on the locus. The synthesis of these special protein tools, like any other proteins, is ruled by a very complex system of organelles inside the cell. Our genes carry the designs for the creation on these enzymes.

To make elastin or collagen, for instance, the cells (fibrocytes) need a huge array of amino acids (AA). Enzymes, being themselves crystalloid proteins, will assemble these AA like beads on a necklace.

Each cell, according to where it is in the body, produces its own crystalloid three-dimensional proteins that activate the creation

---

*Enzyme: late nineteenth cent.: coined in German from modern Greek *enzumos* 'leavened', from *en*— 'within' + Greek *zum* —'leaven'.

or dismantling of organic substances. Enzymes can be stored in a kind of toolbox (lysosomes) in the cytoplasm of cells.

As a tiny drop of salty gelatinous liquid, a cell is not only very complex and well organized, but every action of this internal 'leavening' goes so fast that it verges more towards the speed of light. Enzymes, to be efficient, need a context of heat and co-factors. Just as tools can't construct anything without being in intelligent hands, enzymes don't work without co-factors. A set of vitamins and minerals, oscillating according to the laws of music (and chemistry), is essential as vectors of activation. The laws ruling music, with its octaves of resonance, have much commonality with the laws of chemistry with its octaves of reactivity.

We talk a lot about nanotechnology or machines working with microscopic components. One example is the silicon chips in our computers. Silica is not a semi-conductor so would be useless for computer applications unless it is 'doped' with a very small amount of arsenic or germanium to turn it into a semi-conductor. Our cells are similarly 'doped' with minute amounts of metallic substances that are essential vectors of enzymatic activity. Enzymes and co-factors work in tandem. We are, in the intimacy of our cells, living nano-creatures with a great need for metallic elements in their diluted form. In the next chapter, the Venus Process, we are going to revisit this in more depth where the kidneys play an important role.

Something else is still missing in this story. A foreman on a con-struction site maintains a kind of equilibrium in all the 'brouhaha' of construction. We have tools (enzymes), we have co-factors (oscillating intelligent functions) giving a direction to these tools, and now we need a foreman to bring coherence to all this. The foreman that holds the power of balance are the hormones. They harmonize the complex growth and constant repair. Hormones rule the metabolic processes. Our inner environment works with a multitude of fulcrum points. Health is always a knife-edge expe-rience where too much of this or not enough of that leads to disease. To remain healthy, a specific concentration of calcium, phosphorus, sugar, etc. is needed in the blood stream. These ful-crum points are ruled by hormones.

Scientists today generally accept that the Universe has coherence in spite of its eccentricity: extreme density, heat or vast explosions are often in the news when talking about scientific theory. In ourselves there are similar upheavals but gentler (e.g. fever, rashes, inflammation). Hormones in living creatures, like humour between people, promote easy-going relations. The word hormone comes from ancient Greek and means 'to urge on'. Coming from all the organs they excite our vital processes in one direction or another. They are coded messages that activate only certain cells of specific organs. Most signalling hormones work on a negative bio-feedback loop (see Chap. 1—Drawing 1). One example, among thousands of different ones, is the release of erythropoietin by the kidneys if there is a lack of oxygen in the blood. This hormone will stimulate the red marrow to produce more red blood cells for the blood stream capturing more oxygen from the air in the lungs. Hormones are the essential ruling components in health. Without them there is no coherent growth of organs.

The Mercury Process is about the formation of organs, their constant re-creation and the quality of dialogue these organs have with one another. It is about maintenance, changes and exchanges.

The main hormonal centres (endocrine system) sit along the axis of our lateral bi-symmetry in the area where Ancient Indian tradition locates the seven chakras. It is worth mentioning that organs and their tissues also produce hormones. After all, they are the regulatory messengers that harmonize cellular bio-chemical functions. Organs constantly interact with other organs—using the blood as a postal system or communication network.

B. Lung and its landscape

The Chinese ideogram for the lungs is FEI meaning a plant in a process of ramification, organizing a place between an outside and an inside, covering a large surface of exchange with a network of fibres.

JEAN-MARC EYSSALET (10)

This is an interesting description of the lungs that look like inverted trees (trachea—bronchi—bronchioles—alveolus). The air we breathe is spread over a surface area equivalent to half a tennis court (85 square metres) in our lungs.

Lung in French is 'poumon' coming from the Greek 'pneuma' meaning breath. Without this in and out flow of air there is no internal activation of energy.

> But also FEI refers to the outer skin covering a surface of 18,000 square cm.
>
> JEAN-MARC EYSSALET (11)

> In breathing, the lungs link external nature with human nature. Lungs are like tiny trees made of tiny hollow drops.
>
> HAUSCHKA (12)

The lungs are the organs attributed to Mercury with its globule-forming tendency; the lung microstructure looks a bit like a bunch of grapes (Figure 3—lung unit).

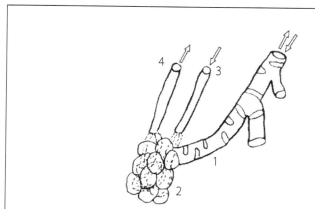

Figure 3: A respiratory unit made of tiny droplets of air

The structure of the lung looks like an inverted tree. The air enters the trachea tube with its cartilaginous rings and sub-divides into bronchi and bronchioles.

1 – The bronchioles, on the other hand, have rings of smooth muscles that can contract or expand the airway.

2 – At the end of the bronchioles are alveolar sacs. They are micro-clusters of individual spherical out-pouching (alveoli). Each cluster is embedded in a network of capillaries.

3 – The pulmonary artery from the heart surrounds these alveoli with its capillaries. This blood, rich in CO_2 delivers this gas to the airway through a pressure gradient.

4 – The oxygen in the airway of the bronchioles passes into the blood stream and exits towards the heart through the pulmonary vein, while the CO_2 exits through breathing out (also with a bit of water). We must not forget that the blood moving out of the lungs has lost water. This is a kind of drainage of the blood. This exchange of gases is very quick.

The cells of the inner lining of the lung produce mucus and are ciliated. The beating cilia direct the undesirable substances (mucus and dust) towards the mouth for expulsion. The pulmonary lining is also populated by huge macrophages (dust cells) constantly processing organic and inorganic dust. If we compare an average cell to a family house, the macrophage in us can be compared to an apartment block.

Rhythmic breathing in and out is ruled by a sensitive area of the aorta. This area senses the content of gases and the acidity of the blood stream, and this information is transferred to the breathing centre of the reptilian primitive brain that initiates the contraction of the breathing muscles (diaphragm and intercostal muscles).

The air we inhale is full of influences that can be partially captured by our consciousness because of our sense of smell. Gases, if we observe them, tend to escape the gravitational pull of the Earth. They expand and exercise pressure on solids. We can contain them in bottles or containers but they penetrate water and biological membranes very easily. Thanks to this action, gases of all kinds permeate us all the time with their energetic qualities: not only oxygen but perfume, aroma and essential oils. Because of their high hydrogen content aromas (the smallest signature of things) invade all living tissues with their formative power (CHI).

When we breathe in, the lungs are in touch with external air. Viewing lung function as a simple gas exchange is a bit short-sighted, however. The air we breathe is carrying diverse climatic influences (dry, cold, warm, damp…) as well as subtle ones (smells and particles of all kinds from flower essences to toxic ones). What about the freshness of the air after the rain has washed the air of its dust (positive ions)? We can breathe a *je-ne-sais-quoi* that we call negative ions. Indian tradition called it 'prana' as a nourishing feature of the air.

The first breath at birth declares our arrival on Earth. At that moment the lungs expand with air and this can be experienced as pain for the newborn, certainly a shock. From that time on we are directly in touch with the outer climate each time we breathe in. It takes several years to harmonize the breathing rhythm with the heartbeat and the movement of the limbs. In the embryo and foe-tus the exchange of gases is accomplished through the placenta, as the lungs are still inactive.

During our lifetime, sensitive cells in the aorta evaluate the content of oxygen, carbon dioxide and the acidity of the blood and send this information to specific centres in the most primi-tive, reptilian part of our brain. It is from these grey matter cen-tres that we unconsciously contract our respiratory muscles. Of course we can also consciously control our breathing.

The lungs are the hardest and coldest of the treasure organs with their cartilaginous bits embedded in the bronchies to keep the airway opens.

The Greek Element Earth predominates in the lung

The life ether is not perceptible directly but can be apprehended by its inner mobility when forms emerge from inside out—like a chick in an egg. It maintains individual totality in space. (See

Note 2 on ethers.) Like the other three Elements, a polarity exists between its state and its ether.

The solid state of matter is made of fixed, immobile volume; made of bits, it can disintegrate and fall into pieces.

The life ether affirms living volumes (organs) and integrates internal metabolic processes. It delineates a contour (skin, bark) according to a living interior, healing and renewing the structure according to morphic fields.

In the past people named the entity of the Earth Element, Gnomes. These life ether entities are the light-filled preservers of the blueprint of creation and live in the dense earth. They are sense-intelligence, bearers of the Idea of the creative universe inside the Earth. Various cultures gave different names to these etheric intelligent entities (see Note 2).

Note 2—on Ethers

Ethers are intelligent activities (entities) that keep matter in movement. The chemical/sound ether, connected with flowing water, were, in the past, called Undines. The light ether, carried by moving air, were called Sylphs, and the Fire Element Salamanders. In Book 3 of *Man and the Medicinal Plants*, Wilhelm Pelikan introduced this subject with Steiner's pictures of elementals and the exercises Steiner suggested to perceive them.

This world of etheric Beings is very close to the physical world. They are essential for the development of living things. Just as the builders of all trades are present in the erection of a house (holding the blueprint of the architect), elementals are there at the beginning of embryonic formation. They work not only in Nature but constantly in us because we are constantly rebuilt. (18) Previous civilizations were aware of these subtle presences and gave them different names such as Djinns, Fauns, GUI. They can influence our mind (especially the life ether entity—gnomes) and our mind can influence them.

Large intestine

At the end of the long small intestine, undigested food enters through the ileocaecal valve into the muscular elastic tube. We don't digest food there, but a complex biotope of micro-organisms starts the final digestive process through fermentation. This U-shape organ has its own sensorial and motor system (brain). We can't digest plant cellulose but gut bacteria can. If the bulk of our food is plants then the cellulose will stretch the tube provoking peristaltic waves. A meal with few vegetables won't provoke a strong stimulation for this organ. It is the workshop organ linked with the lungs. The gut frames the small intestine just as the lungs envelop the heart.

The liquid light flowing in the various meridians of the skin follows a path that goes to feet—thorax—hands—head—then back to the feet. The liquid light in the lung meridians flows from the thorax to the hands between 3 a.m. and 5 a.m. in the morning. Then the flow in the large intestine meridian goes from the hands to the head between 5 a.m. and 9 a.m. Both organs are designed to handle gases. In the lungs it is just an exchange of gases between the internal and external world. In the large intestine the bacteria produce them through bacterial fermentation.

A few words on bacteria and minerals

The concept 'bacteria' didn't exist before the invention of the microscope. We were using them to make cheese, wine … without naming these tiny entities though the Roman Marcus Terentius Varro (116 – 27 BC) and other writers had a certain awareness of them. Varro wrote '…there are certain minute creatures which cannot be seen by the eyes, which float in the air and enter the body through the nose and the mouth, and cause serious diseases'.

Bacteria invade the digestive system with the first colostrum of the mother's milk, and we are constantly in touch with them through food intake (especially lacto-fermented food such as yoghurt and miso). Our first skin contact with them is when we go through the birth canal.

One of the immune strategies we have developed to cope with the constant influx of bacteria through food intake is provided by the stomach. Its acidity is lethal (bactericide) for 'bad' bacteria, or at least bacteriostatic which stops bacteria reproducing and brings them into a dormant state. The bacteria involved in lacto-fermentation (cheese, yogurt, miso, sauerkraut, etc.) are not killed by this acidity. They contract till the end of the small intestine where they are re-awakened to perform their work of fermentation of fibre (cellulose) and other leftovers in the large intestine. They mustn't be active in the rest of the small intestine where we are digesting. We don't want too much gas in there. Whereas in the large intestine bacteria are free to digest what we were not able to process. By doing so they give us vitamins, while freeing minerals caught in the structure of the fibres.

Bacteria are the most ancient form of life on Earth with both plant and animal features. They are not Producers (plant) or Consumers (animal) but Fermentors. Cyanobacteria, for instance, can even disintegrate rock in their association with fungi and algae, creating lichens. No plant or animal can live without a symbiotic connection with them.

We can ask, where do they come from? There is not necessarily a need for an extra-terrestrial origin. They probably appeared in the period when the Earth's surface was too hot to allow liquid water. Can we imagine a time when all liquid water was in the air as hot vapour spreading up hundreds of kilometres? Can we imagine millions of years of strong electric storms bringing heat into the cosmos while cooling the Earth's surface through evaporation? There must have been regions in this very different atmosphere with the right conditions for life to enclose itself in a membrane. Some of these regions must have arisen with a milky composition full of amino acids...influenced by the formative forces of the Cosmos.

Scientists maintain that we have in our bodies far more bacteria than human cells undermining the notion of human individuality. There is no reason to undermine this notion. We just realize that, as earthly living spirits, we live in symbiosis with a second bacterial genome. Initial research in the 1970s seemed to suggest that we might be made up of as much as 90% bacteria! More recent estimates put this figure closer to 50% to 60% bacteria. That still means that over half of the cells in your body are not human ones! And that's not even counting other microbes such as fungi, viruses or archaea.

Often forgotten is the fact that these organisms are so much smaller than even a human cell. If we increase an average human cell to the size of a family house, then a typical bacterium is the size of the door. Viruses are even smaller—the size of the door bell.

Another important factor in our symbiotic relationship with bacteria is the fact that they live at the periphery of our inner empire and our immune system is constantly keeping them at bay and in the right place. In human history, do we know of any civilization that didn't have barbarians at the edge of their empire? In our little interior empire bacteria are the barbarians at the interface between outside and inside. That's why we maintain a sophisticated military presence (immune system with all its fighters and weapons—see Jupiter Process).

Bacteria constantly exercise the activating power of our immunity. We are permanently on the 'qui vive', thanks to the various strategies of our immune system. Bacteria live at the interface between inside and outside (skin, mouth, large intestine, lung, urinary/sexual tract, etc.) and they ferment. By constantly digesting they create an acid environment that is inauspicious for the growth of moulds or fungi (candida, etc.).

The world of bacteria is a complex one. Some are dangerous to human health whereas many are essential. Being the oldest living creatures, bacteria don't store their DNA in a nuclear membrane. For this reason they are called Prokaryotes, meaning that their genetic material is free inside the cell, not isolated in a nucleus. Because of this they seem to have a great facility to exchange genetic material with other bacteria. Some microbiologists consider them as one omnipresent species living in the diverse layers of the biosphere and dismantling everything. They are Gaia's digestive system.

With the development of much bigger plant and animal cells, bacteria were incorporated inside them (endosymbiosis model by

L. Margulis) as chloroplasts in plants and mitochondria in animals. These became little organs in service of bigger plant and animal cells, able to handle energy while keeping their own genetic material. So it is that we have specialized bacteria within most of our cells. Therefore, even many our so-called 'human' cells have bacteria within them. These mitochondria vary in size and shape and some cells have many of them, such as liver cells, whereas some, such as red blood cells, have none. This observation underscores how plants and animals are always in a kind of symbiotic relation with bacteria and that life would be impossible or at least radically different without them.

What do the bacteria have to do with the mineral world? Cobalt, manganese, magnesium, zinc, copper, selenium, etc.... are present in our internal liquids and come in mainly through food. The plant kingdom provides most of them. But plants can't extract these minerals from the ground. They need helpers in the form of bacteria.

At the interface between the root system and the soil, bacteria live in symbiosis with the plants and are equipped to bring these minerals into soluble forms easily absorbed by the plants. Intensive chemical agriculture, where bacteria are not fed properly, generates plants that will have a tendency to lack minerals. There is evidence that GMO plants or plants growing with chemical fertilizers tend to lack minerals. Is it because of genetic manipulation, or simply because most of these crops are chemically produced, that they lack minerals?

Many minerals circulate in us; some are plentiful such as phosphorus, calcium or iron, others are in such a state of dissolution such as copper or cobalt that it took a long time for scientists to trace them and begin to understand their roles as co-factors of enzymatic activity. Other minerals, like lead or mercury, tend to be ejected from the body (through the hair or skin) but leave a trace of their oscillating power with specific properties in our internal liquid.

Plants have a carbohydrate architecture made of complex sugars. When we eat plants we absorb a lot of these complex sugars such as cellulose. We call them fibres and they are essential for the activation of the intestinal peristalsis (fibres give ballast). Each plant cell has a cellulose lining integrated into its membrane. We can't digest these fibres, but the bacteria in our gut can through a process called fermentation.

Through bacteria, minerals go from soil to plants, and in the large intestine minerals go from plants to humans (through fermentation of plant fibres by bacteria). Because of this, the large intestine is an important point of entry for minerals. The skin and the lungs are lesser points of entry. The lungs, framing the heart, and the large intestine, surrounding the small intestine, both handle gases. In a healthy diet only cellulose fibres will ferment producing CO_2. But if we eat too much protein or fat, beyond our capacity to digest them, or if we are not able to produce enough bile or enzymes, then the bacteria in the large intestine will digest the protein or fat producing toxic gases (indol type) that are poisonous and can cause headaches and other symptoms such as damaging the lining of the gut.

These thousands of species of microbes (biotope) living in and on us have been studied by scientists in the last few decades and their healthy impact on our immunity, central nervous system and liver have been observed. And the research continues. It seems that the richer the biodiversity of these creatures the better it is for our health.

Epithelium – a glandular interface between inside and outside

The main tissue separating us from the outside world is called epithelium. The outer layer of our skin, the epidermis, is of this type. Epithelium is glandular, in constant reproduction, and doesn't have blood vessels. It is always attached to connective tissue, rich in blood vessels and nerves that acts as a nurturer and gives elasticity to the epithelium. It is worth remembering that the food we eat is not yet inside our body when we are digesting it. The stomach and intestines are a continuation of our skin and as such, the food might be 'within' us but is still 'outside' of our body. When food is inside this tubular formation it goes through the process of being dismantled.

The digested food is separated by just one layer of epithelial cells before being absorbed into the lymph and blood stream. Again here we have a highly glandular epithelium to interface with the external world between the mouth and the anus. It produces litres of liquid rich in enzymes, mucus and hormones. We have similar epithelium tissues in the uro-genital, lung area and, of course, the highly glandular skin producing hair, sweat and oil. Epithelium tissue is continually renewing itself on a daily basis.

All organs have an interface between an inside and an outside. Some are enveloped in a serous membrane (a glandular mesothelium attached to a connective tissue) such as the pleura for the lungs or the pericardium for the heart. The central nervous system has its complex triple membrane (meninges). Even the blood travels inside an endothelium.

C. Psychic influence: PO

If we consider the importance of hearing and breathing in connection with the larynx for the formation of words and sentences, we find there is also a relationship between the lungs and the living thoughts we want to express. Firmness of thought is one of the motifs given by German anthroposophical doctor, Walter Holtzapfel (1912 – 1994) to the lungs in his book, *The Human Organs*.

The vector of psychic activity in the lungs is called PO in Chinese tradition (13). It is the part of our psyche that relates with the totality of the mechanism of gestation and the YIN nurturing motherly relations to the world. Swiss psychiatrist, Carl Jung (1875 – 1961) called it the 'anima' with a greater interest to transform the inner world than the outer world. There is a corner of our psyche that needs to have a minimum of comprehension of the necessary elements for survival and the administration of our energies and worldly possessions. PO is strongly connected with the instinct of conservation and the cultural life of a territory, be it an individual, a family, a tribe…In some American Indian tribes a woman couldn't be a Chief but it was a council of elder women who would chose the next Chief. This simple fact reflects well the nature of PO. When we put money aside for a future project; when, in the autumn, we preserve food for the winter, when we create a home—rhythmic warm cultural atmosphere…we manifest PO as part of a psychic urge.

If PO has this capacity to assemble energy/substrate to elaborate the vital structures of a species, then who are the builders? What are these organizing forces?

If we look at the meaning of the ideogram PO we have the **radical GUI** that represents a ghost, a phantom with a whirling tail. The vortical tail represents the presence of a vibrant activity in the process of creating organs. It is a kind of vaporous human form. In ancient Western culture men used to see these GUIs as subordinate deities having specific actions—elemental nature spirits. Being the builder of all trades in the natural world, they also are inside us presiding at the constant rebuilding of organs.

PO represents a centripetal dynamic. In this thesis, each human being is a species as such. Its GUI gather and organize the corporeal body just as builders follow a blueprint when building a house. And these GUI are present right at the beginning of the fertilized egg, enchanted in us. PO allows the emergence of species with flesh and passions.

The identification of PO with the creation of organs in the embryo appears very early in Chinese texts. The PO of the forming embryo is one with the PO of the mother. This dialogue allows order in the whole nine months of pregnancy. It is a subtle ordering of the body organs. At birth the lungs of the newborn are activated for a lifetime with its own PO.

PO is linked with an inextinguishable thirst for existence. The 'I AM' that wants to have a tangible body of organs that are given by the planetary force fields we live in. The general external form comes from the living constellations (architects). These morphic fields are dependent in their material expression on the two ancestral genetic lines (male and female). And the whole requires the constant help of these centripetal elemental beings. They work in tandem with the luminous centrifugal power of the creative spirit of the landscapes that invites forces of expansion and refinement of the spirit in us.

> According to these descriptions, the world ether is a manifold activity of many cosmic beings, whose main task is to create the phenomenal forms of the nature Kingdoms.
>
> ERNST HAGEMAN (14)

These formative forces are linked with the four ethers in association with the four states of matter. They don't allow matter to stagnate.

Elementals beings build the soma that gives rise progressively to the psychic faculties—this is why they can influence our thinking, feeling and willing. In turn, our mind can influence them.

With PO we enter the realm of desire but it is a desire to possess things in order to survive. We all need to secure food, drink, shelter, clothing etc. to sustain our life. And this basic survival need to possess things can be exaggerated when, through the accumulation of things, we define ourselves and control others. Then we are caught in a materialistic snare.

This is the negative aspect of this visceral entity called GUI. Any mental rigidity, deep emotional disequilibrium or sexual fixations (pornography) come from the mischievous psychic side of these GUI in us. They have a predilection for any psychic vacuum when the I AM has a weak presence inside the soul faculties. Then they enter this crack and impose their destructive tendencies (i.e. suicide). They long to be disenchanted. We are touching here the foundation of psychosomatic illness. The demons of various religions don't exist outside in a physical sense but reside within us.

There is no way we can control or repress them. Nevertheless the conscious presence in us can acknowledge with reverence their presence and use this tremendous energy to achieve our given talents. The human psyche of today is at an embryonic stage. Scientists are just starting to feel the tremendous power of expression hidden there (parapsychology).

When we look at the decrease of bio-diversity and the destruction of ecosystems through sophisticated technologies, we realize how greedy the human soul can be. Maybe for future generations these last hundred years will be seen as the most barbaric century. With the damage done to Nature and human society, we realize there is nothing to do on Earth but heal—which is Christ's essential message.

Once a building or a machine is finished, the intelligent creativity is not there anymore. With living creatures the forming intelligence is there all the time. Consequently a human being is not a machine, as French scientist, René Descartes (1596 – 1650) maintained. Equating them is ludicrous.

When the I AM is not quite there to make decisions about its destiny, we allow malfunctions in our soul faculties. Then these beings, these GUI will enlarge the cracks because they not only form but can engender psychic deformity.

To become a set of forms, a distinct living body, and obtain a separate inclusive existence with a will to survive, we need the direct intervention of forces of separation—elementals that live in Nature. They are indispensable to weave a human body according to a cosmic blueprint. We are inside a living Solar System that is inside a living galaxy...both reverberate in us. With their centripetal power enchanted into our bodies at the point of conception they shape invisible morphic fields that give us form. These powerful beings (GUI part of PO) have a taste for life and are important in the fabric of Nature to keep matter mobile.

These forces connect us with the sub-world of gravity, magnetism and electricity. This sub-world is a shadow of the supersensible. Of course we are made of electric and magnetic fields but they exist as a consequence of the supersensible acting constantly on the sensible recreating us all the time.

These powers/beings are the same as those used by white and black magicians. It seems that the human psyche can harness them for specific tasks. Also, according to the way we accept our conditioning, our resistance to our destiny, our irrepressible instincts and impulses, it is possible that these elemental beings take hold of an aspect of our etheric vehicle when we die and can manifest as vaporous ghosts. We use elementals to incarnate as separate bodies, and they constantly remind us of the imminence of death—Life is a terminal condition, after all.

Primal emotional reactivity

When we lose dear friends or significant possessions we feel sad. A connection between the past and the present of our life is severed. We share that with the animals. We cry, we grieve.

The lesson of sorrow is let it go, detachment.

D. Metal related to Mercury: mercury

Mercury in nature

Its metal is quicksilver (or mercury) and is the only liquid metal of the planet at normal temperature/pressure with a strong affinity with sulphur. With the exception of a few metals like iron and its relatives, cobalt, nickel, as well as aluminium, quicksilver dissolves metals [like gold] the way water dissolves salts and forms amalgams. It is a very volatile metal that is highly poisonous as a gas.

PELIKAN (15)

Even at room temperature it volatilizes in the air.

Mercury-vapour lamps radiate an intense green-blue light rich in violet/ultraviolet rays.

Mercury has two valences: one is a mercurous compound such as calomel and the other is a mercuric compound such as mercuric chloride.

The main ore is the scarlet-red sulfide of mercury (cinnabar) produced mainly in Europe. As an ore sulphur loses its volatility and mercury its liquidity.

Twice as dense as iron, 14 times heavier than water and with a very high atomic weight, mercury is still a liquid at ordinary room temperature and pressure.

Mercury expands or contracts with the rise and fall of the surrounding temperature (as seen in the column of a thermometer).

Mercury in us

Every organ must be attuned to the totality. It must have a life of its own, but this must not be a self-willed life. Many organs or even cells when cut off from the rest of the organism can stay alive in a nutritive solution. Wherever isolating processes arise in the organism, mercury as a process (not a material substance) leads them back into the fold, harmonizing their activities with the rest of the organism.

PELIKAN (16)

In humans mercury works as a process or vector of activity. With its globule forming tendency, the spherical bubbles of mercury unite when they touch and separate when tapped. Digestion is really a fusion of two spheres—food must be integrated. So it is for respiration (climatic energy meets human energy). As a subtle process, mercury helps to unify external nature with the internal building organs.

Within us, after the external world has been dismantled, the liver starts to rebuild its own new substances. So digestion involves two processes (catabolism and anabolism) and the mercury resonance helps this up-building process to reach a kind of equilibrium. We are not speaking here of the actual substance of mercury but its activity when it reaches a level of dilution.

E. Mercury seal

The Mercury glyph has the Sun symbol at the centre holding the Moon at the top and the Earth at the bottom in equilibrium. It is the only glyph that unites all three.

The external line of the seal is a petal-like shape with less pronounced indentation than the Sun petal seal but still parting the interior. Lines radiate from the centre as in the Saturn seal. They cooperate to develop two sets of serpentine lines that intertwine

with a third line: a shaft with a sphere on top and petal/flower at the bottom. These two coiling central lines support the middle shaft. It is the Caduceus symbol of doctors who try to bring patients into a state of equilibrium, from a state of dis-ease to ease.

We find a similar shaft in the Mars seal but completely encapsulated. The images of the world are captured by the consciousness (the start of psychic life) through pulse motions (Mars). Then they travel in the life of circulation (Sun). Through the Mercury Process the metabolism juggles with organic matter that is in constant change. And so the organs take shape.

'It is Mercury that introduces the substance into the various organs' (17) according to the organ specific line of force (morphic field) coming from the planets.

Health is always in a delicate balance. In its metabolic and psychic manifestations it is a constant dedication to balance. Organs must constantly re-establish a state of balance in regard to the whole and renew themselves. Life consists of innumerable fulcrum points. These balance points have a strong link with the hormonal system, operating mainly in negative bio-feedback loops (see Introduction, Drawing 1 on bio-feedback). We have hundreds of these fulcra in us. The seal shows cohesion in the changing metabolism. Mercurial activity is a constant striving towards a fulcrum.

The ancient Greeks saw Mercury (the Roman Hermes) as the messenger of the gods. The god of doctors, thieves, merchants, and jesters (*le fou du roi*), doesn't allow rigidity. It keeps the 'goods' in circulation. In the intelligent activity of Mercury there is always a certain element of mischievousness—Mercury doesn't allow stagnation, clutter or rigidity.

F. Summary of the lung landscape

Inner organic world
- Treasure organ: lung
- Workshop organ: large intestine
- Associated tissue: membrane (an association of connective and epithelium tissue): the skin
- Energy tendency: drainage and direct meeting with climatic energy
- Vitality of the system of envelopes serous (pleura) or mucus (intestinal lining) membrane providing in-between exchanges
- Dynamic of the energetic system (oxygen for the burning of sugar + the energy of the aroma we breathe + beginning of the circulation of our individual liquid light in the meridians (the energy integrated by the kidney area)

At the skin level the inner world perceives, or insures the health of:
- Flavour and consistency: Spicy, sulphuric food (garlic, mustard), crunchy texture
- Body fluid: nasal liquid and mucous
- Transformed skin: body hair and oily sebum

In the psychic world
- Psychic instrument: PO that assures the management of resources, and energy for survival of family, clan and the cultural aspect of the territory
- Primal emotion: sadness
- Negative feeling: melancholy
- Vocal expression: sobbing, crying
- The health of a perceptual organ: nose, olfaction

G. For the health of this landscape

- It is natural to feel sorrow but beware of self pity and melancholia—they depress this landscape.
- Learn the lesson of letting go.
- Keep the air from getting too dry in winter in the house.
- Be aware of dampness in the house.
- Synthetic furniture, carpets, and cleaning products can emanate toxins.
- Ventilate the house to increase the negative ions and chase the dust out.
- Walk often in non polluted areas and breathe deeply.
- Sleep with open windows.
- Not too much spicy food.
- Eat lacto-fermented food—unpasteurized yogurt, miso— to replenish the gut flora (especially after taking antibiotics). We tend to live in a sterile environment. A strong immunity is observed among people who spend the first years of their child- hood in contact with the natural world. It is a period when the immune system develops at its most.
- Occasional colonic irrigation is good.

References

1 – Rudolf Steiner *Das Geheimnis der Trinitat*, lecture of 28 July, 1922 in *The Harmony of the Human Body* by Armin Husemann.

2 – Rudolf Steiner in *Occult Physiology.*

3 – Ibid.

4 – Rudolf Steiner in *L'Âme Animale*, Berlin, 10 September, 1910.

5 – Ibid.

6 – Rudolf Steiner in *Forming of Man Through Cosmic Influences (Form, Life, Soul and Spirit,* Dornach, 28 Oct. – 5 Nov., 1921, M. Cotterell, translation.

7 – Rudolf Steiner in *Occult Physiology*, Prague, 20 – 28 March , 1911.

8 – Ibid.

9 – Rudolf Steiner in *Occult Physiology*, Lecture 8.

10 – Jean-Marc Eyssalet in *Les Cinqs Chemins du Clair et de l'Obscur.*

11 – Ibid.

12 – Hauschka in *The Nature of Substance.*

13 – The translation of the ideogram comes from Jean-Marc Eyssalet in *Le Secret de la Maison des Ancêtres.*

14 – Ernst Hageman in *World Ether, Elemental Beings, Kingdoms of Nature.* See also *Nature Spirits*: selected lectures by Steiner compiled and edited by Wolf-Ulrich Klunker, Rudolf Steiner Press.

15 – Pelikan in *The Secrets of Metals.*

16 – Ibid.

17 – Rudolf Steiner in *The Planets and their Life Qualities*, Dornach, 29 Oct., 1921.

18 – For more on the subject see Rudolf Steiner in *Nature Spirits* from Rudolf Steiner Press; Jean-Marc Eyssalet in *Le Secret de la Maison des Ancêtres*, from Trédaniel Éditeur; Susan Raven in *Nature Spirits*, from Clairview Books.

CHAPTER 6
VENUS PROCESS

Energized movements for growth
A constant search for the right fulcrum point

Preamble: Molecular architecture

The Beings of Plants through the pulsing activity of the seasons, help create an aspect of the biosphere. Like the hair on our head they go from the Earth or skin towards the air. In so doing, their molecular architecture generates perceptible tastes. In the Spring of their life cycle when the seeds pop out, the alkaline seeds develop **acidity**. Our body continually works hard to maintain the right balance of acid and alkaline substances. Later, bitter compounds emerge. Old dandelion leaves have more **bitterness**, for instance. Plants also produce **sweetness** in their multitude of forms in their seeds and as a reserve in the root system for the winter. We are not talking here about purified white sugar but the sweetness of the aroma of cooking grains (such as when making bread).

With the development of flowers, marking the autumn of their lives, plants go to an intense production of proteins and oils stored in seeds for the future generation. Most of our vegetable oil and protein come from these seeds. **Spicy** substances emerge at this stage: pimento (fruit) or sulphuric compounds in garlic (bulbs).

In their various activities, plants extract minerals from the soil with the help of bacteria. Smell a grated beetroot and your consciousness perceives a mineral content. The most predominant mineral in our diet is table salt ($NaCl$ or sodium chloride). This is a vital element for our internal environment as well as for life in the sea. Besides table salt there are dozen of other salts in us carrying minerals such as magnesium and calcium sulphate. Our body works hard to maintain the right balance of **salty** concentrations and the kidneys are important organs to maintain the various fulcrum points. Similarly, the Earth also has a whole range of strategies to keep a constant concentration of salt in the ocean.

Our consciousness of these molecular constructions (tastes and smells in foods) is due to the sensoriality of our mouth, tongue and nose. The sense of taste can grasp only half a dozen qualities: acid (lemon), bitter (coffee), astringent (sloe), sweet (honey), spicy (pepper) and salt. Acid, bitter and astringent foods tend to dry out (contract) the mouth, whereas spicy or salty food brings more saliva. Some spicy foods, like cayenne pepper can even produce sweat in our face, expanding the membranes.

Once we have swallowed food we are no longer aware of the work these different flavours perform inside our body. These tastes have a direct impact on our digestive system and blood stream and will continue their effects of contraction and expansion, influencing the function of various organs in the body. Flavours are energetic as they impact on the activity of each organ, with a tendency to balance or disturb them. For instance, the Heart Landscape, through the blood flow, represents expansion at its maximum intensity in us. Nowhere else will the blood be shaken so strongly as in the heart. Bitter contracting substances, like coffee, can balance this expansive tendency. Chinese dietetics is based on the understanding of this dynamic balance between the function of an organ and the aromas or flavours that can excite or calm down its activity. (1)

Of course our consciousness of food in the mouth involves also our capacity to perceive their gaseous compounds. That a small patch of nerves at the top of the upper nose, connected to the frontal lobe, can perceive so many aromas is a baffling mystery. And like all gases, these odours penetrate the biological membrane of the nose and lungs and enter the blood stream flooding all our internal liquids. Aroma is the most evanescent signature escaping in the air. People making perfume understand that this molecular architecture has power.

Spending a few hours, walking through forests and green meadows is quite exhilarating. We feel recharged by this sensorial experience, renewed in our too often sedentary bones and muscles, silenced in our busy mental life by the comfort of natural sounds, inspired by the richness of forms and colours. Behind this, however, there is much more going on than what we perceive. There is a complex and constant flow of activities. Our senses perceive so little of the movements of water and sap, the impact of aroma on insects and other animals.

If a feeling of surrender to this living presence (the Beings of things) invades our soul we might perceive, within us and outside an inner sense of balance—'a balance that is not dead but quick with life; we might compare it to a gentle and even flow of water'. (2)

We can't perceive this immediately, but everything in Nature is rhythmically flowing with water as the main carrier.

> And it is the same with every taste, every smell and every sense perception: they inevitably call up in his soul a feeling of inner movement and activity.
>
> RUDOLF STEINER (2)

By scrutinizing the insect or bird world, their movements and activities, we realize that they live in an ocean of scents. Aromas of all kinds come out of the living kingdoms, invade the air in diluted forms; animals perceive and act on these aromas. So it is when observing fishes. The taste/smell of the water stirs them to action.

> Everything in the world of the senses is will, strong and powerful currents of will. I want you to mark this particularly. The man who has attained in any high degree to surrender, discovers everywhere in the world of the senses *ruling will*.
>
> RUDOLF STEINER (2)

Everything in the world of senses is will…differentiated will…

For then, having experienced all the previous (soul) stages leading up to surrender—the stages we have called feeling oneself in
harmony with the wisdom of the world, and before that reverence, and before that wonder—then, through the penetration
of these (soul) conditions into the last **gained** condition of surrender, he **learns** how to grow together with the objects with his
etheric body also, which stand behind the physical body.

RUDOLF STEINER (2)

This is the basis of another methodology initiated by the German
scientist, Johann Wolfgang von Goethe (1749 – 1832). We first
investigate the perceptible world with feelings that open up to the
activities (Beings) of things. It is called contemplative meditation.
Then intuitive discernment is used to separate fantasies from real
imagination.

Venus process: Energized movement for growth: a constant search for the right fulcrum point

A. Life of movement—energizing life
B. Kidney and its landscape:
    the bladder, the bones and red, yellow and spinal marrow
    (brain) and the health of the reproductive system
C. Psychic influence: ZHI + reactivity
D. Metal: copper
E. Venus seal
F. Summary of the kidney landscape
G. For the health of this landscape

A. Life of movement—energizing life

We do have a sense of our own movements. It is due to a multitude
of apparatuses located in the connective tissues of our musculoskeletal system (ligaments holding the bones, tendons attaching
the muscles to the bones, muscular envelopes for the cells, etc...)

sending messages to our brain. We become conscious of the location of our limbs, their speed of movement and stretching capacities because of these sensorial organs.

In this chapter on the Venus metabolic process, we are talking about movement but something totally different from the sense of movement. We have animated forces that work in us in the intimacy of our cells. The blood flow circulates the blueprint of our organs (Sun Process). Then the substances are trapped into lines of force and fill the morphic fields in a balanced way (Mercury Process). And now, with Venus, another action takes place in the intimacy of each cell—the work of innumerable living droplets of gelatinous cells. What happens in these drops of salty jelly is very complex, well organized and functions at a speed close to the speed of light.

For instance, we all live completely 'doped' with a specific ratio of micro-quantities of minerals, vitamins, etc... in our liquids. Minerals are important activators of enzymes without which no metabolic movement can happen. Biochemists call them enzymatic co-factors. These minerals are like the masters of ceremony as they control and trigger many processes. But their organizational properties work only if they reach the right level of dilution. Here the minerals are hardly material anymore but energizing essences. In electronics we use the semi-conduction of silicon. But silicon has no semi-conductive property by itself. It has to be 'doped' with a very precise amount of a mineral (arsenic, germanium)—then we have movement.

Other more complex substances play a similar role in us, such as colour pigments and vitamins. The growth process is unthinkable without these micro-quantities of substances coming from our food, and acting as vectors of all enzymes functions.

We eat pigments all the time like chlorophyll from vegetables or hemoglobin from meat. Pigments often carry a metallic nucleus. Our own body also produces pigments such as rhodopsin in the eyes or melatonin in the brain.

> They [minerals) may be conceived of as energies not yet in a state
> of material fixation, forces capable of forming complete healthy
> protein by their harmonious interaction.
>
> RUDOLF HAUSCHKA (3)

Nineteenth century chemists started to see the human body as a
heat-powered machine, a kind of factory. They looked at living
entities as complex mechanical devices. This picture is still here
today in the minds of many in various scientific fields. But the
word vitamin originally comes from that era when chemists had a
presentiment of the existence of substances working as oscillating
energy more than coarse matter.

With these micro amounts of substances we stand beyond the
theory of calories that reduces proteins, lipids and glucides to
simply a quantity of heat energy. Minerals or vitamins are not
part of our structure. They act in small amount and sometimes
just the oscillating process is present. Organs dose these substances all the time, and the kidney landscape is at the forefront of
this activity. As we saw in the Sun Process, it is the function of the
heart to potentize (succuss) these diluted substances. The kidneys
and bladder, with the impact of hormones, are the main diluters.

> Through metals we can act deeply in the intimacy of our internal
> universe. But the external activities of substances that combine
> easily with air (volatile substances) can exercise their raying out
> on the whole organism, even in the blood and the totality of the
> organic systems.... And you can see that we have opposed only
> now the activities of the human organism with the mineral inor-
> ganic nature of salts, vaporized metals and the substances easily
> combustible [aroma].
>
> RUDOLF STEINER (4)

This is an aspect of the Venus Process as energizing force.

B. Kidney and its landscape

The kidney ideogram includes the servant (or minister) of a prince, kneeling down and also a hand holding firm the people under his command. There is also an image of flesh attached to the ideogram that represents an organ determining firmness. In this context we have an organ presiding at the realization of the individual form through a growing process from foetus to adulthood. The kidneys combine all the subtlety between what needs to be diluted in the fluidity of our pulse liquids and the living rigidity of our bone structure.

In the plant kingdom the seed production is a return to the essence—a contraction point where the plant can start a new cycle. The kidneys, seated at the back behind the floating ribs, have a bean shape. They are outside the peritoneal membrane with the bladder and the sexual organs. Like the other organs, the kidneys have their own protective layers: the renal fascia that holds the kidneys in position behind the floating ribs and the adipose and renal capsules. Through the kidney-bladder link, blood flow is contracted constantly. Several times per hour the blood goes back to its essence—a ratio of substances needed to maintain life.

> It is the renal system, in a way, that harmonizes the external influences, as a result of blood—air contact, and internal influences coming from the digestive process.
>
> RUDOLF STEINER (5)

To understand this sentence we need to ponder a bit on the meaning of external and internal influences. With the Saturn Process we saw the role of the spleen as a gatherer of subtleties from the fine oscillating tones of food and air. These, too, have to be integrated.

The smell and taste of things have a mysterious subjectivity for scientists. They can't put a mathematical finger on them. The fact that the essence of lavender, for instance, has a calming effect on our psyche, prompting relaxation or sleep, is just an example of an aroma influencing our biological system. Essences are types of energy as they generate a biological effect.

While the material side of food undergoes a destruction process (catabolism), and at the same time begins to rebuild in the liver (anabolism), the subtle essences of air (YANG CHI) and food (GU CHI) are captured by the *spleen aerial* (see Chap. 1—Saturn Process) and brought down to the *kidney sphere* to mingle with our own ancestral energy (YUAN CHI) to create our unique liquid light circulating in the meridians and in our other moving liquids (blood, lymph and cerebrospinal fluid).

This is the basic energizing movement of the Venus Process that allows growth and constant renewal.

The kidney area is like a sanctuary lamp constantly powering our individualized liquid light which is essential for any bio-chemical functions (see Note 1 (liquid light) in the Introduction and Drawing 1 in Chap. 3).

From this new mix, our individual liquid light (KHEN CHI as Chinese tradition called it) is ready to flow up like a surging fountain towards the **Heart sphere** (see Sun Process) and spread through all the meridians and moving liquids (blood, lymph, cerebrospinal fluid). This energetic system is called the Triple Warmer in acupuncture, and is a YANG integrator like the digestive system. Then the Master of the Heart—as a YIN distributor like the circulatory system—starts to carry this transformed energy over a period of 24 hours.

The entry point of that circulation in the meridian is the beginning (No 1) of the lung meridian on the skin of the thorax. The law is simple in physiology: *what enters us must be made our own.* This circulating liquid light is the stimulator of all bio-chemical processes (see Drawing 2 in Chap. 3—Mars).

Note 1: On Quantum

At the end of the nineteenth century, scientists in their fragmenting search of the infinitely small discovered that the atoms are not the ultimate un-dividable constructions but are themselves built of components. It was found that some atoms like radium can decay emitting various frequencies to become another element. That was the beginning of the study of these elusive particles or 'quantums' of energy.

Realizing that matter is actually made of various condensed packets of energy (quantum) they imagined experiments to study their uncanny behaviours. At the same time, studying the infinitely great cosmos they realized that the Earth is constantly bombarded by ionizing radiations ranging from ultraviolet to cosmic rays. Suddenly the empty space between the stars became completely filled with particles of all kinds. Quantum physic was born in an attempt to grasp mathematically this strange phenomenon.

On the other hand a book was published in 1908 by the Theosophical Publishing House called *Occult Chemistry*. A. Besant and C. W. Leadbeater as leaders of the Theosophical Society at that time, cultivated a yogic technique that allows their conscious mind to descend into the infinitely small atom of each element and slow down this vibrant world to see the various particles making their architecture (c.1900). Their investigation predicted some new elements not known at that time.

The ANU (C6D4) was described by these authors as the ultimate particle—in fact there are two, one turning clockwise and the other anti-clockwise. They are lovely beating heart-shaped vortices.

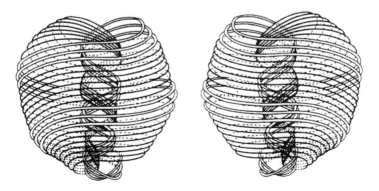

Figure 1: The two ANU

Rudolf Steiner never contested their theosophical findings but did scold them for working only in a materialistic way at the ultimate fragmentation of matter. He said that they should have asked: where do these strange atomic constructions come from? What are the formative entities behind them? Then they would have had to turn their gaze towards the pulsing star systems and consider the progressive evolution of the Earth.

In 1980 the American theoretical physicist, Stephen M. Phillip wrote a book called *Occult Chemistry Revisited* where he stated that the magnification and description of atomic forms in Besant—Leadbeater's book is pretty coherent with the modern understanding of theoretical physics.

Photosynthesis in plants, semi-conduction in our connective tissues or piezoelectricity in our compressed bones are quantum phenomena because they involve movement of particles be it a photon or an electron. Nevertheless, the *currents of liquid light* in our meridians as well as our thoughts and the phenomenon of consciousness are not quantum phenomena but are etheric in nature. Thought forms as well as currents of liquid light have a constant impact on our bio-chemistry which is connected with movement of particles between substances (reactivity).

These currents condense themselves to a point where they grasp the material substance of the body in order to make organs. We have the impression that streams of *clear ethereal light* [liquid light] *go from one organ to another and flow in the whole human organism.*

RUDOLF STEINER (6)

The Greek Element Air predominates in the kidney

That is why Steiner suggested that the kidney area is auspicious to understand the Greek Element, Air (gas state of matter (12) and the light ether (12)) because it predominates in the kidneys. Gas state and light ether are polar opposite.

Gas state: fills the space between objects, compressible, elastic, without structure. Creates pressure on solid objects and penetrates water and biological membrane in its expansion tendency.

Light ether: reveals objects by separating them, linear oriented tendency, divisible, breakable. Space, forms and colour are made visible.

If we pass an electric current through a tube that has a rarefied gas then the gas lights (fluorescence). There is then a connection between gas, light and electricity.

An aspect of the light ether is perceptible by our eyes. It is the colour frequencies of the electro-magnetic spectrum. Nevertheless sunlight, beside carrying heat and light, is loaded with the formative blueprint of creation coming from the constellations and the planets behind it. The Sun, as Steiner pointed out on several occasion, is a three dimensional black hole in the fabric of space/time (see Reference 1 in Chapter 4—Sun Process). So are the other Suns of the Universe. Like holes in a black canvas they allow the spiritual light to pour into the dense world. In their movements across the sky, there is always one of the twelve constellations behind our Sun in this dynamic clock we are living in. The Sun exercises a sucking effect, bringing down these formative forces (from both constellations and planets). This is the other aspect of the light ether. *Sunlight reaches us also by reflecting on the moon and the planets.*

The Chinese medicine movement called WATER reflects the function of the kidney. The WATER ideogram means a return to the original state, like a seed which is the origin of all forms. The WATER ideogram is associated with the phenomenon of condensation, concentration, solidification. What the blood is experiencing in the kidneys (contraction) is similar to our experience of night and winter, on a daily and seasonal basis. By a simple decrease of light and warmth, the whole of Nature around us condenses (dew), contracts. That is exactly what the kidney is doing to the blood. It concentrates the diverse substances, dilutes them according to the needs of the species and sorts out what is no longer needed. Through urine we lose heat, gases, water, and a multitude of minerals and organic substances. In animals and human beings the kidneys/bladder always play an important role in keeping this ratio balance right for the species.

The kidneys, like the brain, are organs that consume a huge amount of sugar and oxygen to operate. When sugar is consumed in muscles, the energy released gives heat and movement. In the kidneys and the brain the energy released doesn't emanate heat but light. In the brain this energy is essential for the nervous influx (bio-electricity) production. In the kidneys this energy rebuilds the blood stream to its contracted essence. Being part of the Triple Warmer the kidney sphere, also produces a 'clear etherial light' that the ancient Chinese called KHEN CHI which is the mingling together of the subtlety of air and food with our ancestral energy.

Heart (FIRE movement) and kidney (WATER movement) work in tandem, the first bringing expansion to the blood, and the second bringing concentration of substance. The kidneys constantly dilute substances, and the heart, in its shaking of the blood, creates millions of vortices bringing the oscillation of a substance into the micro-structure of blood/water. Often the side effect of allopathic drugs on organs is due to the fact that they are too acid or bitter and also too difficult to break down and eliminate.

The unique ideogram called YUAN CHI

Concerning YUAN CHI, our own unique ancestral energy, the Chinese understanding of the *concept heredity* contains several aspects that make each human individual a species by itself.

First the word ancestral means not only father and mother but also their mother's and father's genetic make-up for several generations. This genetic make-up is only one part of what the Chinese call heredity.

Second, what is in the blood stream and the psyche of the parents around the moment of conception will have an impact on the male and female gametes that make the zygote. Twenty ovules and millions of sperm are involved in fertilization. They live in nourishing liquids from the blood stream which is a summary of physical and psychic activities. These will have an impact on the winning sperm and ovule.

Third, the nine months inside the mother's belly with what she eats and lives psychically.

Fourth, the birth process.

Fifth, the first seven years of life experiences, which are of vital importance (cultural heredity).

After four years there is a kind of energetic lock when the communication between the central nervous system, the immune system and the endocrine system are set for the whole lifespan. Any physical or psychic trauma during these first years seems to have a detrimental effect on the way these three systems (primal adaptive system) dialogue with one another. The more the physical and psychic environment of the family or tribe is made of loving, welcoming rhythms, the more this system is a promoter of health.

At birth the embryonic brain will develop through tender sensoriality, so it is important that there be no 'bulimia' or overstimulation of sounds or images. Free motricity to explore the world is another imperative for the building of the link between the brain and the muscles. The limbs part of the metabolic process (*will*) is very predominant at that age. We perceive a strong will in a child to explore the world while expanding in space.

Also if a toddler doesn't hear a human language in the first four years, that's it: the brain centres for language must be stimulated during that period or they don't develop.

Bladder

The kidney-bladder complex, every minute of our lives, creates the right ratio of minerals and organic substances by contracting the blood (through excreting urine). It is important here to see the bladder not simply as a bag temporarily holding urine. The bladder is an organ that penetrates the kidneys with its multitude of tentacular vessels. These vessels meet the blood stream at the glomerular apparatus and form a nephron (see Drawing 1). We have a million nephrons for each kidney. There is the same penetrating tubular effect in the relation between the gall bladder and the millions of hexagonal structures of the liver (see Jupiter Process in Chap. 2).

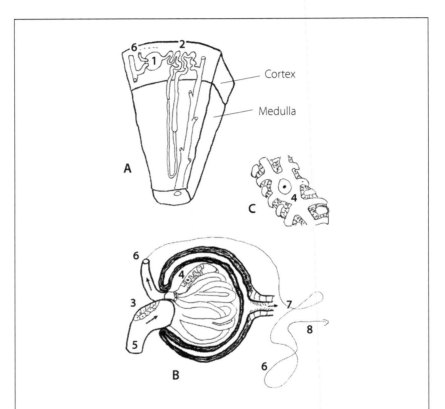

Figure 2: Nephron and its renal corpuscle

Nephron and its renal corpuscle

There is a continuity of structure between the bladder and its numerous tubular extensions into the kidneys. In Chapter 3—Mars we looked at the gall bladder and saw a similar formation where the gall bladder's tubular system enters deeply into the lobules of the liver. In that case the tubes carry the bile that is transformed in the gall bladder located inside the lower part of the liver.

In this instance, the tubes extending from the bladder to the kidneys are surrounded by capillaries that the urine will progressively form around. Chinese tradition considers the bladder as the workshop organ of the kidney.

A – A general view of one nephron. There are one million of them in each kidney. We must imagine the bladder tubules completely enmeshed in capillaries (not shown) coming from the artery (6),

B – An internal view of the Bowman capsule (10). Here the bladder tubular system becomes a capsule allowing the arterial blood stream to create a multiple loopy perforated capillary system. It is unique that an arteriole vessel turns into a capillary bed (inversion) and goes back to an arteriole which then develops a new capillary network around the bladder tubes.

C – Each capillary loop is tightly surrounded by cells (podo-cytes) forming a kind of kidney/blood barrier. In the capillaries of the brain we have a similar arrangement where the astrocytes, nursing the neurons, are part of the brain/blood barrier.

1 – Each Bowman capsule initiates the start of the urine formation. In the emergence of the Bowman capsule we observe an interesting phenomenon. The capillaries 'invert' themselves into loopy structures pushing the end of the bladder tube into a gastrulation gesture forming the double layer membrane of the capsule. It is between these two layers that the blood abandons most of its substances. This is the juvenile urine that is carried away by the beating of the ciliated cells of the bladder tubes. In the description of the Venus seal we will once again see this gastrulation/inversion process.

2 – Beyond the capsule we see a complex and convoluted pathway of bladder tubes going down and up between the cortex and the medula of the kidney (Henle loops). These

tubes are surrounded by a matrix of capillaries. It is in this relation between these tubes and the capillaries that the blood is reconstructed with the help of hormones, various pressure gradients (osmosis) and nerve inputs from the autonomic nervous system. This allows the rebuilding of a specific ratio of substances in the blood. Most of the juvenile urine is re-absorbed (99%). Around one litre of blood passes through the kidneys every minute, but we produce only around one litre of urine a day.

3 – There is a small area of the arteriole entering the capsule that is forming the juxtaglomerular apparatus with the proximity of the distal tube of the bladder. It is composed of sensitive cells that respond to low blood pressure by releasing an enzyme (renin). This renin provokes a cascade of reactions involving the liver and the lung that will bring more water into the blood stream. It is called the renin-angiotensin-aldosterone response and is very important in the maintenance of the right blood pressure.

4 – One podocyte enveloping a capillary in a tight embrace filtering the blood.

5 – The arteriole brings the red blood into the capsule to be filtered.

6 – The arteriole leaves the capsule, having lost most of its constituents and becomes a matrix of capillaries around the bladder tubules. It is from this dialogue between capillaries and tubules that the reconstruction of the blood occurs.

7 – The blood serum (urine) is directed towards the bladder tubules with beating ciliated cells. After the serum is reshaped it goes to a collector tube (9) leading towards the bladder as such.

8 – Finally the new contracted blue blood exits the kidney towards the renal vein.

It is worth mentioning that the kidneys, like the brain, consumes a huge amount of sugar and oxygen to operate but don't emanate a lot of heat. It is all about light transformation whereas in the muscle, consumption of sugar and oxygen is all about movement and heat.

In the glomerular apparatus the blood abandons most of its constituents to the bladder canaliculi and is rebuilt with the help of a complex set of hormones, because for a while the bladder tubes are surrounded by a matrix of blood vessels.

The kidneys-cum-bladder dry the blood. In fact the blood flowing out of the kidneys has lost heat, gases, water and a whole range of organic as well as mineral substances. This is our urine. We have here a contraction process that leaves in the blood only what is essential. Our urine is not necessarily waste but the excess of that we have in the blood stream. It is a permanent uncluttering. Like the seed for a plant, the recreation of the blood is a return to its essence. Blood flowing out of the kidney-bladder, with its new balanced ratio of substances, undergoes this return thousands of times a day. This is the YIN aspect of the kidney sphere or glomerular filtration that brings the blood stream into its seed essence.

The bones and their marrow

Bones are the most contracted crystalline organs on our body. Their level of density provides a frame that supports all the other organs. Each bone with its envelope (periosteum) is alive with blood vessels. Bone structure appears early in the embryo as cartilage that little by little ossifies in the most marvellous concentric way. Every one of us builds a unique skeleton as the hardest image of our higher self.

Short headline

1 – The entry of a blood vessel in the cylindrical structure of the compact bone (Harversian system).

2 – The osteocytes that deposit calcium phosphate and collagen fibres. These cells expand their membranes in such a way that they all touch one another (up/down—left/right—front/back) forming a unified matrix which is in constant communication as a functional unit.

When a bone breaks the osteocytes become osteoblasts and start the re-unification according to the morphic field of that bone.

Figure 3: Concentric bone structure of long bones

The inside of long bones are hollow and filled with a yellow marrow, a rich oily substance stored there as a treasure—our own vital reserve.

Areas inside bones (ends of long bones, sternum) present a spongy configuration. In this space live the original stem cells constantly renewing the blood cells (red and white blood cells). We call this area the red marrow.

These two marrows are defined as something inside bones. There is another marrow: the spinal cord or 'spinal marrow' as the French refer to it. It is inside articulated bones (vertebra and cranium) and includes the brain. Like the other marrows the central nervous system is mainly fat. The phospholipid substance is predominant there.

The varied concavity and convexity of the bones are moulded by the muscles attached to them. They grow together in the foetus—the tendons fixed to the bones are not glued there but, when approaching the bone, the cells of the tendons (fibrocytes) become bone cells (osteocytes). This whole architecture shows a beauty of proportion coupled with function.

In the absence of gravity, as with the astronauts in space, bones tend to disintegrate. In our ordinary life, with weight bearing or muscular activities, the crystalline structure of bones is stretched and compressed and produces a kind of piezoelectricity (see Note 2 in Jupiter Chapter 2) that stimulates the osteocytes to produce more calcium phosphate and collagen.

If there is no physical exercise and no pressure from gravity on our bone structure they don't produce piezoelectricity. Many crystals, when compressed, emit this form of electricity and the bone structure is no exception. When excited by exercise the bones compress, twist, stretch, etc., activating the osteocytes.

Bone density depends on the use of them. An extreme example is observed in various martial arts such as Karate: a person hits a hard surface with the side of his hand repetitively every day. The result will harden not only the skin with calluses but the structure of the hand (bones, ligaments and tendons) by depositing more structural substances (calcium phosphate and collagen). The hand doesn't get bigger but heavier, becoming a more powerful weapon.

Because the concentration of calcium and phosphorus is so important in the blood stream, a specific hormone (parathormone) around the larynx area induces cells (osteoclasts) to liquify bone matter while other (calcitonin) hormone stimulate cells (osteocytes) to rebuild bone matter.

The kidney-bladder landscape is on the contraction (winter) side of the five movement cycles (return to the essence). The long bones and their cavities that contain our basic ancestral reserve of energy (yellow marrow) is part of this landscape. It is said that when we die of old age there is no more yellow marrow inside the long bones. Inside bones we also have the red marrow responsible for the creation of blood cells. The spinal marrow (spinal cord/

brain) is also inside articulated bones (vertebrae and cranium) and like the other marrow is very rich in fat (60% phospholipid). The brain depends on minerals diluted by the kidney/bladder and succussed by the heart. The brain tissue operates greatly on minerals of all kinds, and it is the kidneys that balance them. The cerebrospinal fluid in touch with the grey matter has a mineral content with various level of dilution.

The health of the brain depends on this kidney landscape. The brain, like the kidneys, operates on sugar and oxygen. No heat comes out of burning sugar in these organs. But when muscles burn sugar (glycogen) we have movement and heat. The burning of sugar in the kidneys and brain produces light, bio-electricity and substances. Chinese medicine called the kidney area the Sanctuary Lamp because it constantly produces the liquid light (YANG aspect of the kidney).

There is a hormone (hematopoietin) produced by the kidneys that increases the creation of red blood cells in the red marrow if oxygen is missing in the blood.

> Yes, freedom consists in moving the muscle/bone structure in the external world. He isn't free who follows his impulses and instincts. A free man rules himself by the requirements of the external world that he must learn to love and with which he must establish a relationship. All that expresses itself through the imagination of the bone structure. It is the muscular-skeletal movements that capture the living thoughts (imagination)…that is why there is a correlation between physical work and cognitive imagination. …The fact that I, as a child, split wood, harvested potatoes, dug a garden, planted seeds, etc., has enormously contributed to my imaginative faculties.
>
> RUDOLF STEINER (7)

The sexual organs

Like the kidneys and bladder, the sexual organs are outside the peritoneum and connected with the kidney sphere. Like the kidneys that contract the blood, sexual organs generate gametes (a contracted potential) that can be used to invite a friend from within. Designed in the animal kingdom for the reproduction of the species and strongly controlled by pheromones, in human beings this survival centre is greatly extended to human relationship and ecstatic pleasure. It is amazing, over human history, what lengths mankind has always gone to access this moment of ultimate relaxation. From harems to brothels, from mono to polygamy, so many books have been written and the subject is never exhausted. It still haunts us because it is the seat of fantastic creative energy embodying an aspect of God the Father, and at the same time open to degradation (pornography).

This sublime centre of activity hasn't been mastered yet by humankind. Vampirism is not only about drinking the blood of others but about sucking out their life forces through untimely sexual activity (paedophilia). In the chapter on the Mercury Process we discussed the elemental beings building us constantly and their mischievous tendency on our psyche. Some work more at the metabolic level and can distort our Will faculty. The demons of Christian and other theologies are not something outside us but within us. People addicted to porn are actually under the spell of GUI that always wants more of the stuff—it becomes an addiction or a possession.

A word about reproduction

It is amazing how many different children can come from the same couple, one mother and father—not only physically but genetically different with different aspects of their parents. Many creatures, like most of our cells, can just divide into two for reproduction (mitosis)—this is called cloning.

As for the other aspect of reproduction (meiotic division), where two ancestral lines mingle their genes, we end up with a set that represents an aspect of the genome of that species. Ovaries and testes produce gametes (ovules and sperm), and each time it is a half of the essence of that creature. When fertilization occurs it is a unique gene assemblage because it never happened before and will never happen again. And so it has the sting of death as far as that specific combination of genetic material is concerned. This began very early in the evolution of living creatures.

Example: if you go to an orchard with only one variety of apples you can be sure that no two trees have the same combination of genetic material. Every tree is a unique expression of the genome of that species. The foundation for this cosmic tendency is in the formative forces of the Scorpio constellation. (8)

C. Psychic influence: ZHI

In the context of the kidney/bladder energetic landscape, this specific creative spirit is called ZHI. It means a drive, a psychic creative force in direct relation with the concrete realization of the talent/potential of an individual. A child, like a seed always brings preferences to explore the world in his own way. In the kidney sphere we are, in a condensed form, a contracted summary of the strengths and weaknesses of our genetic make-up, whereas at a psychic level we are a summary of the strengths and weaknesses of our cultural heredity. Beyond genetic and cultural heredity a child always brings his own preferences to explore the world. As the German doctor, Walter Holtzapfel (1912-1994) says in his little book, *The Human Organs*, the kidneys lend vigour to the temperament.

The whole ideogram refers to a capacity to realize a destiny. It can be seen also as a will force that can gather momentum towards the fulfilment of a heart aspiration. The ideogram also means an arrow touching its goal with the radical for the mouth. This last image represents a will force that allows one to speak about a subject with the precision of a directed arrow touching its target.

The will of ZHI does not direct our ordinary daily psychic activities. It is more visceral. It is the drive that governs specific behavioural activity and survival strategies. For human beings we need to add to this animality what we bring from other incarnations and can be summarized by a will to realize a personal destiny.

The German philosopher, Arthur Schopenhauer (1788 – 1860) makes this distinction between '*Wille*', a will below the consciousness and '*Willkurk*', a reflected will determined by conscious motivations (personality). ZHI is this *Wille*: a primordial thing engendering the body (embryo becoming a foetus). Another German philosopher, Immanuel Kant (1724 – 1804), also saw this *Wille* as the ultimate foundation of all phenomena including all the internal, unconscious organic functions. The whole animal body is a creation of *Wille* entering into space. There is always a complete concordance between the *Wille* of a species and its body organization. (9)

Primal emotional reactivity

This kidney landscape (Venus) contracts the blood into its essence like seeds and buds in plant. Fear as a primal emotion contracts us too. Fear is a reaction to a potential threat to our individuality. A danger to our psychic or physical integrity will contract our internal environment. With deep fear the blood withdraws from the skin. We become as hard as rock. We might even pee in our pants as the bladder contracts.

Between foolhardiness (absence of fear) and phobia (constant apprehension), the human psyche has to find a point of balance. The cultivation of trust which is done through the Higher Self (the conscious presence in us) is a good start to overcoming fear and cultivates courage.

D. Metal related to Venus: copper [10]

Copper in Nature

Copper is not only versatile in its association with other elements but is very colourful.

Most copper ore lies near the Pacific Ring (Chile), but a subtle distribution of it can be found everywhere on Earth.

It is chemically so active that it combines with most other substances, including sulphur and iron.

It fluctuates like iron between two conditions of reactivity—uni-valence (cuprous salt) and bi-valence (cupric salt).

Copper is one of the few substances to have such colourful beauty as an ore.

A dynamo for electricity production is made from a highly purified combination of iron and copper.

Copper in living beings

The Echinoderms (starfish) and other Invertebrates use copper pigment to produce strong brilliant colours.

In humans it is an essential co-factor in the creation of colour pigments (haemoglobin, melanin) as well as in the plants for chlorophyll.

Copper has a great affinity with water, sulphur and proteins that makes it ideal for life.

Copper is used as a 'breathing metal' in lower animal kingdoms (oyster, crab, snail), just as we use iron in our haemoglobin.

Copper chloride, when crystallizing, can be an indicator of formative forces in organic liquids such as blood and sap (sensitive crystallization).

The planet Venus is strongly linked with the number five due to the dance (five loops) it performs around the Earth over a period of eight years. The Echinoderm is the only animal phylum showing a symmetry based on the number five.

In plants, a trace element of copper is essential for the formation of chlorophyll. In animals and humans a trace of it is needed for the formation of haemoglobin. It is slightly more abundant in the substantia nigra of the brain with its melanin-containing nerve cells.

The vitamin B group, responsible for the construction (anabolism) of organic substances, doesn't work properly without the copper co-factor. We saw earlier that Venus is involved in the growing and maturing process, so we see why its concentration in the human blood is carefully maintained.

Lower living forms, such as mould, blight and fungi, are inhibited in their growth by traces of copper.

When highly potentized in homeopathy, copper is recommended for exhaustion/fatigue because it increases the regenerative process.

E. Venus seal

The periphery is made of two wavy lines reducing the petal shapes that we see in the Sun and Mercury seal. The external and median lines follow one another and show internal cave-in movements that delineate the expression of the internal line.

Starting from the centre, the seven internal lines move towards the periphery with an elegant gesture showing gastrulation/inversion at their extremity. We have at the top of these volumes a **gastrula** concavity holding a convex bud **inversion**. If we look at the embryonic development of many structures in us, we see this form. One example is the brain ventricle development that transforms the blood into a salty, mineral-rich, warm, oxygenated and clear liquid that feeds the grey matter and gives buoyancy to the brain as well as maintaining a pressure gradient on it.

> Inversion takes place from physical, gravitational space into the etheric counter space of light.
>
> ARMIN HUSEMANN (11)

Due to this process of inversion that creates the brain, our outer impressions become thought forms. *This an aspect of the energizing power of Venus.*

In his book, *The Harmony of the Human Body,* Armin Huse-mann (German Dr. b.1950) writes:

Physical organic tissue is extended by the etheric body.

Bi-dimensional in nature, the etheric invites the formation of a surface/envelope—skin, mucus or serous membrane.

Physical organic tissue is invaginated by the astral body.

Because this astral vehicle is tri-dimensional in nature, it invites the formation of volumes/organs that express planetary metabolic processes.

Physical organic tissue is inverted by the ego-organization.

This Ego entity aspires to go beyond the gastrulation to access new dimensions.

The eyes and the cranium are, among others, examples of a gas-trula stage (forming inner cavities for organs) going to an inver-sion step. (11)

(See Drawing, Note 1B in Chap. 5—Mercury.)

Every living creature sculpts a form in space through a time pro-cess. It is in the volume/organ/flower of the plant that the meta-bolic process is at its maximum activity. Most of our vegetal proteins and oils come from the flower area. In animals and human beings there is a cosmos of proteic volume/organ. In the seal, the seven independent vessels, tightly packed and formed by an internal line, touch each other in a harmonious way like organs in tune.

In the Sun script the internal space in completely open. Here we have several closed spaces. The external and median lines form one virtual space. This underscores an important physiological law: all organs and organisms are isolated inside a surface/envelope/membrane, often serous in nature like the pericardium and the pleura with a virtual juicy liquid space. The internal irradiated lines form seven independent spaces, closely related vessels. The other closed space is between the periphery and the central line.

If in the Mercury Process the organs materialize according to morphic fields, in the Venus Process the organs, well encapsulated and harmonized with one another, play out their energizing movement of growing and maturing through gastrula and inversion.

F. Summary of the kidney landscape

Inner organic world

- Treasure organ: kidneys
- Workshop: bladder
- Associated tissues: bones and marrows: yellow (reserve), red (blood cells production) and spinal (instrument of consciousness)
- Energy tendency: contraction. Return to the origin
- Vitality of the marrow including the nervous substance (spinal cord, brain)
- Dynamism of the genetic (sexual organs) and energetic system by the creation of our individual liquid light (KHEN CHI).

At the skin level the inner world perceives, or insures the health of:

- Flavour and texture: mouldy, mushroom, juicy consistence
- Body liquid: urine, non-enzymatic saliva
- Transformed skin: hair

In the psychic world

- Psychic instrument: ZHI—strength and weaknesses of ancestral energy coupled with talents and potentials received and the will to achieve
- Primal emotion: fear
- Negative feeling: phobia, panic

- Vocal expression: groaning
- The health of a perceptual organ: the ear (hearing and equilibrium)

G. For the health of this landscape

- Beware of irrational fear (phobia) as well as foolhardiness (a caricature of courage).
- Live your potential and talents with gusto.
- Do not isolate yourself or become too passive.
- Acknowledge both the feminine and masculine aspect of the psyche.
- Do not eat too much salty food. Like sugar, salt is used as preservative—read the labels.
- Use conflicts with friends and partners to work on your own shadow.
- Keep warm in cold weather, especially at the back—the kidney is already a contracted organ.
- Express sexual energy inside a loving relationship so as not to deplete this landscape.
- Birch leaf decoction on a daily basis was recommended by Steiner for people in the autumn of their life (over 50 years old). This tree is assigned to Venus by the old tradition. Throughout our life our body constantly renews itself but beyond a certain age the degenerative process is more prominent. The Venus Process reverberates in birch leaves and favours growth and rejuvenation for a gentle ageing process.

References

1 – This living relation between sensorial perceptions and organ activities was of great interest for the ancient Chinese physiologists. Their reflection on the subject is exposed in the book, *Dans L'Ócean des Saveurs, L'Intention du Corps* by Jean-Marc Eyssalet, edition Trédaniel. This is the basis for Chinese dietetic where the healing occurs through the flavours of food that calm the hyper-activity or stimulate the hypo-activity of an organ.

2 – Steiner in T*he World of the Senses and the World of the Spirit,* Hanover, 27 December, 1911 – 1 January, 1912.

3 – Rudolf Hauschka in *The Nature of Substance.*

4 – Steiner, *Occult Physiology,* 28 March, 1911 (GA 123).

5 – Ibid.

6 – Ibid.

7 – Steiner in *L'art de guérir approfondi par la meditation,* Dornach, 8 January,1924.

8 – See *The Mystery of Emerging Form* by Yvan Rioux, Temple Lodge.

9 – Schopenhauer in *De la Volonte dans la Nature,* p. 78.

10 – From *The Nature of Substance* by R. Hauschka and *The Secret of Metals* by W. Pelikan.

11 –*The Harmony of the Human Body,* Armin Husemann, Floris Books, 1994. Here he describes the discovery of 'Gastrea' by Ernst Haeckel, as well as Steiner's exercises with clay, to experience inversion which is the embryonic continuation of the gastrula gesture. In this book Husemann applies musical principles as a method of gaining insight into the structure of the human body and the forces that work in it.

12 – Ernst Marti in *The Etheric,* Temple Lodge.

CHAPTER 7

MOON PROCESS

Replication (mitosis vs meiosis)
Self-renewing life

Preamble: In search of coherence

The Austrian-born American physicist, Fritjof Capra (b. 1939) in his book *The Tao of Physics* was among the first to attract our attention to the similarity between the search for new paradigms with the discovery of the behaviour of particles (quanta of energy) and the way the ancient people of India explained the World. Decades of expensive scientific research with sophisticated instruments pushed away the notion of the fixity of atoms. Atoms were found to be constantly on the move and unstable—their components, the particle, unpredictable.

From the solid foundation rock of our perceptions, in the space of a few decades, scientists' model of the world shifted in such a way that we actually don't know the majority of the matter that makes up the Universe—scientists simply refer to this missing mass in the Universe as Dark Matter and Dark Energy. On the other hand, a long time ago in India meditation had yielded a similar interpretation of the Universe: human consciousness can access the coherent inter-connectiveness between the physical world and other dimensions, everything that happened in the past is recorded (Akashic record).

What were they tapping into? Is it time now to reckon with a new phenomenon beyond matter and energy? This thesis tends to show that the emergence of the soma (organic structure) from a single cell generates progressively a psychic world that is not just complex bio-chemical activities. The human psyche has powers of expression that can't be explained by the old scientific paradigm where everything is merely matter and energy. Let us imagine that the brain does not produce thought forms but reflects them to our consciousness in the same way that a radio doesn't produce programmes, it just captures radio frequencies and translates them into sound. If this were the case, who is the broadcaster of our own thought forms? What is consciousness anyway? Our psyche, for sure, has ways to recreate the world through language, artistic expression and survival skills, but who is there using these faculties, these 'knowing how' to transform the perceived world? The idea of a self-conscious presence (Spirit or Entelechy) at the threshold of soma and psyche is an interesting and important notion.

The America journalist, Lynne McTaggart (b. 1951) in her book *The Field* has collected some laboratory observations of psychic capabilities. Several para-psychological phenomena have been confirmed as substantial observations. From telepathy to slowing down radioactive decay, from bending spoons to projection of the mind over distance, we are just beginning to uncover new intriguing properties of the psyche in relation with matter. Of course these observations don't fit with the current paradigm of the scientific world view. For conventional scientists it is tempting to say—'I've made up my mind, don't confuse me with the facts.' Observed facts are the first step in any honest scientific enquiry.

Even more puzzling is the observation of the elusive world of particles in sophisticated experiments where the psyche appears to relate with them. Quantum Physics in particular poses problems as a field of study as it seems that the scientist can no longer be an objective observer—the very act of observing and measuring affects the experiments. New concepts emerge to put a handle on their activities: non-locality, entanglement, string theory, holographic memory, hyper space, phase relation, information field, 'A' field wave, multi-dimension space, unified quantum vacuum... the list goes on.

And the search continues for coherence which is a natural attribute of the human mind. Nature is a fine-tuned interconnected whole. The more we unveil new properties of matter the greater the temptation to describe the human being in the light of these new discoveries. Books have been written describing man as an electric machine with a holographic memory behaving as a complex computer. It is even tempting to see consciousness operating at a quantum frequency level.

The Hungarian philosopher of science, Ervin Laszlo (born in 1932) in his book *Science and the Akashic Field* wrote, 'the quantum field appears to link all parts of the organism ... and it may also link the whole organism with the environment'. It makes sense, knowing that the connective tissue has semi-conductive powers—meaning electrons move along a matrix of highly organized crystalloid proteins all over the body with a sensitivity to what is going on inside and what comes from outside. Nevertheless, the liquid light flowing in our meridians is not a quantum phenomenon. It is etheric in nature, beyond the realm of particles, like psychic activities, but by acting on our bio-chemistry it generates an electric and magnetic field that can be measured with the right equipment.

For Laszlo the evolution of the Universe has no fixed goal but a definite coherent direction. For him every single event, every human deed is recorded in the quantum field and never lost, his 'Akashic field' which he equates to the 'Zero Point Energy' concept of Quantum Physics. He sees the whole Universe as a mega computer—'a kind of supersensible organism'. In this paradigm the Universe is more a vast reservoir of coherent thought forms summarizing previous happenings. There can be moments of material deconstruction (chaos) but nothing is ever lost of previous achievements and a new Universe can start again tapping into what happened before. In this model there is no place for the evolution of individuality.

It took a long time for us to accept the fact of natural progressive evolution even if the modern theory of evolution still has a long way to go to explain it. Due to missing links between phylla and major destruction of species in evolution, we need to posit some periods of major creative leaps such as the Precambrian explosion. How long will it take to accept that each human being is on a journey here from incarnation to reincarnation? How long will it take to accept that the Spirit world, creating the Physical world allows the emergence of a Psychic world which is itself in touch with the Spirit world? Are these three worlds actually co-evolving together? Here we are at the boundary of matter and the spirit—a difficult place to integrate in a materialistic era searching for coherence.

The philosopher and mathematician, Alfred North Whitehead (1861 – 1947) stated that the world is made of coherent intelligent processes, a kind of 'society of actual entities', well integrated and interacting with the whole of the physical universe. The whole has coherence.

Moon process: Replica (mitosis and meiosis)

A. Life of reproduction—Self-renewing life
B. Part of the kidney landscape. Centrosomes organizing the duplication (mitosis). Moon Process and meiosis
C. Creative spirit part of the kidney landscape
D. Metal: silver
E. Moon seal
F. Summary of the kidney landscape—see Venus Process
G. For the health of this landscape—see Venus Process

A. Life of reproduction—Self-renewing life

Two forms of reproduction occur in living beings. The first one involves a mitotic process where a mother cell divides into two daughter cells generating two genetically identical cells (clones). From bacteria to our own dividing cells, this form of duplication prompts the creation of two mirror images of the original cell. This is an aspect of the Moon Process. It is the Cancer impulse that produces an enclosure (1) through its material aspect, phosphorus. Phosphorus is instrumental in the creation of highly sensitive and motor cellular membranes. Considering the important role that cellular membranes play, we might discover that they are in fact the 'brain' of the cell rather that the nucleus as is sometimes assumed. (2) Cancer's ruler is the Moon which makes sure this little drop of interiority is perennial through self-replication (cloning).

The second form of reproduction starts with the meiotic process where only half of the genetic material is present. It appears also very early in the evolution of species. It has to do with the exchange of half the genetic material of two individuals (male/female gametes) leading to the creation of a unique genetic make-up related to the genome of its species. This meiotic process happens in specific organs (pistil/stamen in plants—ovary/testicle in animals). Unlike mitosis this process has more plasticity; the sector of the Milky Way responsible for it is Scorpio (3) promoting embryonic development with a unique set of chromosomes.

The Moon Process also has an impact on this second form of reproduction. The menstruation cycle is close to 28 days (the span of the moon's waxing and waning). These cycles of the moon also have an impact on the movement of liquid in plants and animals and, concordantly, influence the human reproductive cycle (the most fertile time is the middle of the cycle). The Moon cycle will also affect the psyche in various ways. It is well known that people with a mental disability are more unsettled during full moon periods. Hence the word lunatic from the latin *lunaticus* meaning 'of the moon'.

The area responsible for both forms of duplication is called a centrosome. It regulates the life cycle of all cells in us. It is a dense spherical area pretty close to the nucleus made of peri-centricular material (PCM). Inside this dense area there is an organelle called micro-tubule organizing centre (MTOC) responsible for all internal movements: the centriole (see Drawing 1). This little organelle is as ancient as cellular life on Earth; it hasn't changed and has to do with rhythmic internal cellular movements. A cell is a dynamic living nano system whose inside is an isolated colloidal droplet of liquid with a highly organized skeleton of fibres linking the organelles together with the nucleus and the outside. (4) Like the mitochondria, the centriole has its own genetic material which is different from its host. The four main activities of these cylindrical proteins is connected with movement.

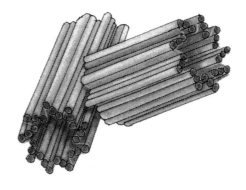

Figure 1: A Centriole 'tube' made of triplets of groups of nine '**tubulins**'.

A – In plant and animal cells centriole orchestrates reproduction. In animal cells the centrosome contains a centriole made of two little barrels sitting at right angles to one another. These barrel-tube shapes are axially constructed with an array of nine tubulin triplets (Drawing 1). Tubulin is a kind of cylindrical protein initiating movement. At the time of reproduction, when everything seems to fall into chaos, the centriole migrates and determines two poles in the cell, giving it order and orientation. The poles connect together with a network of tubular filaments where the chromosomes will duplicate at the equator of these two poles.

B – The same nine tubular triplets of proteins are part of the interior structure of cilia and flagella initiating movement.

C – The centrosome is the main organizer of the tubular matrix of the cytoplasm (cyto-skeleton). Cells, as small droplets of salty colloidal water, orchestrate the production of proteins, and this matrix facilitates the transport of substances at a very high speed.

D – As we saw earlier the axonal elongation of the neurons not only carries bio-electricity but is full of tubular proteins helping the axonal transport of substances. As semi-conductors, like all other connective tissue protein fibres (collagen, elastin, etc.), these tubular networks can also carry information (sound, bio-photon) through a process that doesn't involve a bio-electric current but semi-conduction.

Tubular proteins are everywhere in the cells. There is a great degree of coherence within this micro tubular matrix. With semi-conduction powers, bio-photons as well as piezo phenomenon can travel these tubular pathways and communicate with all the cells. Cell activities operate close to the speed of electricity. We can see that part of the processes in the body, including cell communication, is triggered by 'quantum fluctuations'. The other part of the processes (etheric aspect) has more to do with the production and circulation of the etheric liquid light explained in 'Venus', Chapter 6.

At this stage we can ask: Why do we have tubular structures? What is a cylinder? Why do we have nine triplets of tubulin proteins coming together in a larger cylinder (centriole)? Why are three and nine so important in organizing these intra-cellular movements? One characteristic feature of a tubular shape, be it made of wood or metal, is its ability to produce and channel sound waves. From organ pipes, flutes, drums or wind-chimes, the tube shape is key to creating music. These tube proteins live in the liquid realm of the body and have a connections with the chemical/sound/music/number ether.

Cells have many functions and one of them is to reproduce when needed in the organ where they live. For various reasons (chemical substances, radiations) sometimes the cells in an area start to reproduce non-stop without any consideration for the morphic field of the organ. We then have cancer that can be benign or malignant. This rebellion against the coherent whole happens all the time, according to oncologists, and our immune system can usually get rid of these rogue cells that run amok.

We are living in a more and more polluted environment that seems to stimulate anarchy in some weak parts of our body. This pollution takes many forms, from atmospheric pollution of our environment to nutritional pollution of our increasingly artificial diet through to electromagnetic pollution with ever increasing radiation continually surrounding us. Although massive research focuses on battling new and increasing numbers of cancers, very little is said about how to increase our immunity.

When looking at potential problems in our bodies at a cellular level, we must inevitably come to viruses. Often thought of in the same breath as bacteria, viruses are actually very different. Typically much smaller than bacteria, viruses are not really alive in any traditional sense and there is still some debate in the scientific community about how they should be regarded. They are a tiny DNA segment encapsulated in a proteic capsule that can enter the cellular membrane. When not in contact with a cell a virus will not use energy, reproduce or clearly react to its environment, leading some scientists to label them 'biological chemicals' rather than living organisms. Viruses always need a cell to reproduce. When it comes in contact with a cell, however, it captures the cell's equipment to produce multiple duplicates of itself. By doing so it kills the cell and invades other cells. Sometimes the dying cell has time to produce a substance (interferon) that tells other cells how to stop the intruder. In the case of a cold or flu virus, it takes around a week for the immune cells to create specific weapons to fight the virus.

One big challenge with viruses is their capacity to change their genetic material from one year to another. Bacteria and plants have their own viruses that don't affect us. Animals and Human Beings share similar viruses and sometimes they can interchange genetic material. We have seen some dangerous outbreaks of previously unheard of diseases that have seemingly jumped from animal to human populations—such as 'Bird-Flu' and 'Swine-Flu'. If animals under stress in intensive farms lose their vital space, their immunity decreases and they are more likely to lose the continuous battle against viruses, potentially creating new or more virulent strains that might then pass to their human handlers.

The 1918 flu pandemic known as Spanish Flu is widely viewed as one of the deadliest natural disasters in human history likely responsible for the deaths of over 50 million people around the world. Much research has been done to ascertain its cause and origin and much remains unknown. One thing is clear however: the events of the First World War, with hundreds of thousands of people in wet trenches for months on end with chemical weapons and associated supply chains of livestock and poultry were the ideal breeding ground for the H1N1 influenza virus to spread. In much the same way as our over-reliance on antibiotics is now creating super-bacteria, human actions such as wars and intensive farming practices may well be creating super-viruses.

B. Part of the kidney landscape

See the Venus Process

C. Creative spirit part of the kidney landscape

See the Venus Process

D. Metal related to the moon: silver

In nature

The Moon reflects the Sun and its metal is silver (Ag), which we use to make mirrors and photographic plates (silver chloride).

Silver is the most colour-sensitive metal and the best heat and electric conductor. It is very soft and flexible and is an alkali metal.

In us

All metals, except iron (the lightest of the seven related to the planetary processes), work in us only in very small quantities. Their material side is not so important; when they are diluted their subtle oscillations start to manifest. These vectors of activity have an enormous impact on the speed and orientation of the enzyme tools that build proteins.

> The essence of a living organism lies not in its substance, but in its action. Our organization is not a system of substances. It is activity.
> Rudolf Steiner (5)

Silver activity is more on the up-building side of our metabolism.

The Moon is our closest planetary body and associated with the metal silver. Saturn is the furthest away [in this sequence] and is associated with the metal lead. The planets beyond Saturn are seen, in this work, as having mainly an effect on our psychic life. These two metals oppose one another in different ways. Silver is an alkali (base) and is the most ringing of metallic tone. It gleams brilliantly, melts only at high temperature and has the highest degree of conductivity of heat and electricity. It is exactly the opposite for lead. [Silver] is also highly sensitive to light (photographic process).

RUDOLF HAUSCHKA (6)

Silver's properties are an earthly condensation of the Moon forces. Its process, when silver is present in a very small amount, is the force responsible for all these life rhythms like budding, germinating, reproduction (renewal of species). It happens that silver is everywhere in nature and in the ocean (10 mg per cubic metre).

RUDOLF STEINER (7)

The Liesegang ring phenomenon helps to round out our picture of silver and of the inner mobility that accounts for its reproductive power. When a drop of silver nitrate falls on a glass plate coated with chrome gelatine that has not quite hardened, the silver reacts with chrome. A round reddish-brown spot of silver chromate appears. It spreads in all directions, not in the even way an inkblot does, but in wave after wave, each one of which makes a concentric red-brown ring around the original spot. What is characteristic here is the rhythmic repetition that forms concentric spheres where one might have expected to see just a single sphere as the spot spreads out. There is outflowing motion with a rhythmical wave impulse like the spread of a musically vibrating sound. This is another example of the kinship between chemical forces and music; the chemistry of a substance is like an inner music that organizes matter into ordered patterns.

WILHELM PELIKAN (8)

The Liesegang rings recall the concentric ripple patterns that spread out in rhythmically expanding waves from the place where a stone is thrown into still water. We might call both reproductive.

RUDOLF HAUSCHKA (9)

E. Moon seal

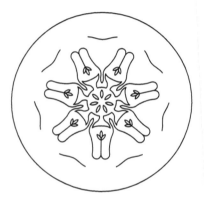

The peripheral line, as in the Mars seal, is reduced to much smaller pulsating wings.

The seal shows a similarity with the Mars seal in the sense of contraction and confinement of a shaft with three petals.

Moving inwards, a continuous line creates the containers of these leafy shafts.

The third line surrounds the centre with seven chalice-like gestures that penetrate the second line container. These chalices receive the confined leafy shaft. Each chalice has a secluded place inside the middle line container. There is a suggestion of intimate intercourse.

We have a fourth set of lines irradiating droplets/seeds from the centre as in the Sun seal. If, in the Sun seal, these droplets represent the free circulation of formative and pictorial sense impressions moving from outside in, here in the Moon seal these droplets suggest a reversed movement going from inside out. Because of the intimate inter-relation of the middle line with the third line, this inwardness suggests the fertilizing gesture that creates new seeds into the inner sanctum of living creatures.

F. Summary of this landscape

See The Venus Process

G. For the health of this landscape

See The Venus Process

References

1 – See *The Mystery of Emerging Form* by Yvan Rioux, Chap. 1—Cancer constellation (citing your own work is frowned upon—but sometimes necessary).

2 – See *The Biology of Belief* by Bruce Lipton.

3 – See *The Mystery of Emerging Form* by Yvan Rioux—Scorpio constellation.

4 – See *Energy Medicine* by James L. Oschman, Harcourt Publishers Limited, 2000.

5 – Rudolf Steiner and I. Wegman in *Fundamentals of Therapy.*

6 – Rudolf Hauschka in *The Nature of Substance.*

7 – This quote by Steiner is taken from *The Nature of Substance.*

8 – Wilhelm Pelikan in *L'homme et les Plantes Médicinales.*

9 – Rudolf Hauschka in *The Nature of Substance.*

Conclusion

A planetary alignment giving birth to our physical and psychic world

The etheric world is a bi-dimensional (points, lines and surfaces) world that builds layer upon layer all the various surface membranes of living organisms. These membranes produce niches for organs to develop and exercise their function in harmony with the whole. These organ volumes, the basis of the astral body, are the resonance of the Planetary Spheres in us. Directed by the Planetary Spheres' morphic fields, our stem cells differentiate in various loci and generate organs following lines of force. We exist in a living cosmos and the Planetary Spheres of influences reverberate in our inner cosmos.

This is the thesis of this book that tries to give a provisional answer to the questions:

What determines the biological form and function of our organs? What external forces affect those organs? In turn, how do these physical affects on our body impact on our own inner life especially with regards to the development of our inner world, our psyche?

Both Rudolf Steiner and traditional Chinese medicine had a lot to say on these questions and their ideas are explored extensively in the text.

The soma — the emergence of the body structure

Chapter 1 – Saturn—opening the door of perception

Our sense apparatuses on the surface of our body (eyes, ears, skin etc...) are designed to grasp an aspect of the world which will be revealed to our consciousness.

The spleen/pancreas-stomach/duodenum landscape starts to free the subtle resonance of food and integrates the various external rhythms touching our lungs and skin. The integration of the external world with our own inner bubble has begun.

Chapter 2 – Jupiter—establishing and defending an inner territory

The nerve system preserves what has been captured by the senses. It is the beginning of the brain as an instrument for consciousness in this dense world.

The liver-gall bladder landscape is at the start of the creation of our own inner territory (surface membranes of the connective tissues) and its defence. Several substances help to re-enforce the immunity (turmeric...). Also our heart enthusiasm for what we do in life is an important factor. This bio-chemical pathway is well known. Enthusiasm, like being in love, stimulates the thymus to produce thymosin which is an important hormone for awakening the lymphocytes B and T. They develop the tools for getting rid of what is not 'us' (cancer or even an organ transplant). This landscape is also the beginning of the creation of our own proteins for immune protection and hormone efficiency. Animal starch (glycogen) for movement, and bile for an efficient digestion, are also part of this landscape.

Chapter 3 – Mars—the beginning of a psychic world

Various pulsations and membrane tension around our grey matter make us conscious of what has been perceived by the senses and preserved by the nerves. The Beings of things become pictorial in our mental activity forming our everyday psychic world.

The strong bile concentrated by the gall bladder facilitates the dismantlement of food. Every complex food needs to go back to its primitive dissolvable form (amino and fatty acids, glycerine and simple sugar). By doing so the JING CHI = vitamins, minerals, aromas, pigments ... as co-factors of enzyme activity are free to operate in the cells.

Chapter 4 – Sun—the diffusion of organ pictures

The perception of the Beings of things circulates in the blood stream as a stimulant for the planetary morphic fields of our organs. What was pictorial for the psyche becomes formative for the soma.

The heart-small intestine landscape is at the forefront of the distribution of influences, as the blood and its vessels go into the intimacy of each organ. This pulse unfoldment is nourished by the milky chyme that is absorbed by the small intestine.

Chapter 5 – Mercury—from a flow of formative pictures to material organs

This is a world of constant changes where the organic substances flow into one another following morphic fields. This needs aroma and oxygen to be constantly at the right concentration through ventilation (pulse motions). The realm of healthy metabolism is defined as a constant knife-edge experience.

The lung provides the necessary O_2 and CO_2 exchange for the freeing of locked energy in the cells and handles the subtle influences of the air. On the other side, the large intestine frees minerals and vitamins through the bacteria digesting cellulose. This is an anaerobic composting process that produces gases.

Metabolism comprises destruction and construction. All this intense metabolic activity is kept at various fulcrum points with the help of the hormonal system working in a negative bio-feedback loop. It is a feature of the Mercury Process to establish this equilibrium. Most of these hormones come from the glandular aspect of the epithelium tissues. The master glands (endocrine system) sit along the axis of the vertebral column, but in fact each organ emits its own hormonal messengers to rule various areas of the body. Cells have a capacity to sense and respond to these messengers because of aerial-like features (a kind of individual fingerprint) at the surface of their membranes.

Chapter 6 – Venus—energized movement for harmonious growth

At a material level we know various substances that act inside the cell in very small quantities. Biochemists call them co-factors of enzymatic activity. In their states of dilution their oscillating power organizes the enzymes and their speed of reaction. We are doped with them. They are the various micro quantities of minerals and vitamins that we receive with our food. Again, their precise balance is vital to our health and always being monitored and adjusted by various processes in our body.

The kidney-bladder landscape constantly contracts the blood stream to its primal essence bringing these energizing co-factors, hormones into the right ratio of substances in the blood of a species.

At an energetic level, Chinese physiologists remind us that everything coming from outside needs to be integrated into our own substance. The air and food contain their own oscillating power (aroma) that has to be digested just as food is in the digestive system. But aroma like any gas expands and penetrates the blood stream. They have to be processed by another digestive system (the Triple Warmer). The kidney landscape has an important energizing role here. The subtle resonances of food and air captured by the spleen go down to the kidney area and mingle with our unique resonance given to us by our parents (ancestral energy or YUAN CHI). A new mixture is formed called ZHEN CHI (our personal liquid light) that emerges like a surging fountain towards the heart to invade the meridians and various moving liquids (blood (rhythmic pulse), lymph (digestion—defence) and cerebrospinal fluid (brain = neuro-sensorial) on a daily basis. This energizing movement is the basis of all bio-chemical activities. This system that integrates the subtle influences of food and air is called the Triple Warmer (YANG—integrator) and the Master of the Heart (YIN—distributor). This system has no specific organs but lodges in areas of the thorax and abdomen where the five landscapes inter-relate.

Chapter 7 – Moon—self-renewing life

Most cells can renew themselves through simple division of a mother cell into two similar daughter cells. In some areas of the body it is a daily occurrence (skin) whereas other cells, like the neurons, can't reproduce because they are lacking the centriole. Nevertheless the original cells (stem cells) are still lurking dormant in our tissues and can be awakened when needed. A lot of research today focuses on this question of how to activate them for self-renewing specific areas of the body.

Of course, the ancestral desire to produce progeny reverberates at a sexual level where half of the genetic material of a male and female mingles to form a unique chromosomic ensemble. This mode of perpetuation started millions of years ago in plants and animals. This process is called meiosis and features a once-only combination of genes. This is a gift from the constellation of Scorpio (1) that allows us to invite a unique friend from inside out. To this individuality we may give cultural and moral imprints learned mainly through imitation, but a child also brings challenges for the parents. He doesn't come as an empty urn but has aspirations (ZHI) to express and talent/potentials.

The psyche—the emergence of an inner world

Each of the five landscapes has its own metabolic process that governs our inner territory and this resonates in the building up of our psychic life. (2)

The confusion that reigns in modern physiology comes from thinking of the soul as an emanation of the nervous system… Man, as a being of soul and spirit, transforms and redirects the substances absorbed by him in ways we have as yet only dim premonitions. (3)

Each set of organs has its own creative spirit providing the basic framework of our psychic ability: YI for spleen, HUN for liver, SHEN for heart, PO for lungs and ZHI for kidneys. As observers of any living system, the ancient Chinese saw no differences between the human body make-up and the organization of their society—another living unit. That is why they attributed social titles to the organ systems. There is nothing in the fabric of society that is not present in the living matrix of our own interiority.

1 – Through the **Servant of the Heart** (Spleen—Saturn sphere) the creative spirit (YI) gives us the mind that can gather ideas, memories, insights and delivers them in a coherent way (language, artistic expression). The whole fabric of the Universe has wisdom and the human mind has been in a constant search for coherence; the mind is constantly in search of an ideology that turns what is perceived into a comprehensive coherent unity.

2 – Through the **General of the Army** (Liver and gall bladder—Jupiter and Mars sphere) the creative spirit (HUN) is a self-assertive power that transforms the outer world for survival, creates a territory and defends it for the realization of a destiny. It has a YANG transformative power that manifests through craftsmanship. It is the energy of the birthing process.

3 – Through the **King of the Kingdom** (Heart—Sun sphere) the creative spirit (SHEN) stays in touch with the spiritual dimension. It is the site of global intuitive intelligence and our insight comes from this capacity to stay in touch with the spiritual world. This reverberates in the brain so that our consciousness can grasp it. The heart is a dwelling for the Higher Self. Knowing that, the ancient Egyptians mummified the heart with the musculoskeletal system but no other organs. This SHEN spreads all over the body through the warmth of the blood. Too much heat (fever) or not enough (shivering) seriously impairs our capacity to use our soul faculties.

4 – Through the **Prime Minister** (Lung—Mercury sphere) the creative spirit (PO) is more exploring (anima) the psychic world in progress than the outer world. This is the ground for cultural stability in any group—the YIN (listening) relation to the world that tends to preserve the social cohesion and renew it. PO is the gestation period of our embryonic development and up-building

where the GUIs or Elementals work in the construction of our body. These GUIs, as intelligent craftsmen keeping the states of matter in movement, can have a negative effect on our soul faculties. They are enchanted in us and long to be free. GUIs can impact our soul faculties and lead us towards dogmatic thinking and negative feeling, such as hatred or obsessive sexual activity (pornography). These negative tendencies can affect our vital function. There is a longing for these entities to be free again and they can be mischievous. As far as life is concerned everything rigid is on its way to extinction.

5 – Through the **Sanctuary Lamp** (Kidney—Venus sphere) where the fire of our ancestral energy burns, the creative spirit (ZHI) reveals into our consciousness our innate talent/potential with the courage to realize our specific uniqueness. This is the centre that harbours the strengths and weaknesses of our genetic and cultural heredity and holds the etheric flame to feed the SHEN (Higher Self) on its path of realization.

Note on seven planetary metals presented

As suggested by Steiner, we work with a planetary sequence in order to enter into a better comprehension of the seven metabolic processes or life stages.

In *The Secrets of Metals* the pharmacist, Wilhelm Pelikan organized a circular heptagonal sequence **based on the atomic numbers** of the metals related to the planets. These numbers show an increase in atomic weight starting with iron, and proceed left with copper, etc. He knew that 'our inner cosmos is permeated by metallic activities'. Several hidden links were discovered in connection with our organic threefoldness and the days of the week.

Regarding the factfiles on planetary metals presented here, we can say, with Pelikan, that the inner planets have more to do with our **metabolic pole** (Moon/silver—self renewal, Mercury/mercury—the appearance of physical organs and their maintenance through hormones and Venus/copper—energizing growth through the right balance of co-factors of enzymatic activities).

On the other hand the outer planets stimulate our **nerve sense pole** (Saturn/lead—sensorial organs, Jupiter/tin—the nerve preserving the sensations and Mars/iron—the pulses that allow pictures to touch our consciousness). In the **rhythmic pole** we have an intermediary mix of metals with gold at the centre: Mars/iron—the use of energy through the capture of oxygen; Sun/gold—circulation and Venus/copper—harmonious growth.

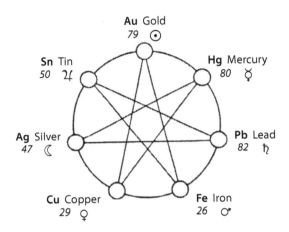

Heptagonal sequence of planetary metals

References

1 – Chapter on Scorpio in *The Mystery of Emerging Form* by Yvan Rioux, Temple Lodge.

2 – The translation of the ideograms of the creative spirits of the five landscapes is from Jean Marc Eyssalet in *Shen ou L'instant Createur*, Guy Trédaniel Éditeur.

3 – Rudolf Hauschka in *Nutrition*.

Recommended books:
David Lorimer—*Beyond the Brain*
Denis Noble—*The Music of Life—Biology Beyond Genes*
E. L. Grant Watson—*The Mystery of Physical Life*.

The Mystery of Emerging Form
Imma von Eckardstein's Drawings of the Constellations
A Biological Perspective
Yvan Rioux

Contemporary science views our planet as an insignificant speck of dust in the vastness of space, with its four kingdoms as a random assemblage of atoms. Yvan Rioux presents a radically different perspective, demonstrating an indissoluble relationship between Heaven and Earth. Over aeons of existence, the four kingdoms have manifested a creative power that perpetually brings forth new expressions. With the goal of bridging science and spirit, Rioux helps revive the old intuitive awareness of an intimate communion between the outer perceptible life of nature, the inner life of the soul and the majestic spiritual formative forces that preside as architects – an organic whole where all levels co-evolve.

The earth, nesting in its solar system, is connected with the Milky Way and the twelve constellations. The impact of the stars as an influence on human behaviour has been known for millennia. In the original edition of Rudolf Steiner's *Calendar of the Soul*, twelve illustrations of the constellations, made by Imma von Eckardstein, were published for the first time. These intuitive drawings differ greatly from the traditional ones, but Steiner stressed their importance for our modern consciousness. The images invite us to comprehend formative forces in their various guises in the kingdoms of nature. By exploring the gifts of each constellation, the author uses Imma's drawings as a template to elucidate the emergence of twelve basic forms as the common denominators of all creatures, leading eventually towards the human form.

'The [new] images of the zodiac constellations represent actual experiences connected with the waking and sleeping of particular spiritual beings. In these images we have a knowledge that needs to be renewed at this time...' – Rudolf Steiner (1912)

April 2017; 196pp; 21.5 x 13.5 cm; paperback;
ISBN 978 1 912230 02 0; £16.99

TEMPLE LODGE

A note from the publisher

For more than a quarter of a century, **Temple Lodge Publishing** has made available new thought, ideas and research in the field of spiritual science.

Anthroposophy, as founded by Rudolf Steiner (1861-1925), is commonly known today through its practical applications, principally in education (Steiner-Waldorf schools) and agriculture (biodynamic food and wine). But behind this outer activity stands the core discipline of spiritual science, which continues to be developed and updated. True science can never be static and anthroposophy is living knowledge.

Our list features some of the best contemporary spiritual-scientific work available today, as well as introductory titles. So, visit us online at **www.templelodge.com** and join our emailing list for news on new titles.

If you feel like supporting our work, you can do so by buying our books or making a direct donation (we are a non-profit/charitable organisation).

office@templelodge.com

TEMPLE LODGE

For the finest books of Science and Spirit